Reach For Your Spiritual Potential

by
Doris Black

QUALITY PUBLICATIONS
P.O. BOX 1060
ABILENE, TEXAS 79604
(915) 677-6262

ISBN: 0-89137-438-8

Dedication

*To Jack,
my constant source
of encouragement.*

The Church of Christ
Tuscumbia, Alabama

Table of Contents

Chapter One
God's Vision For Us

When we are born into Christ, we are just a radiant promise of what we can one day be. A promise of unfulfilled spiritual potential. But even then we are more than conquerors, for nothing, "... *neither death nor life, neither angels nor demons, neither the present nor the future, nor any powers, neither height nor depth, nor anything else in all creation, will be able to separate us from the love of God that is in Christ Jesus our Lord ...*" (Romans 8:38,39). In the same way nothing can keep us from reaching the spiritual potential God has planned for each of us—nothing that is but us. The trials and burdens of life may slow us down, spiritual battles may sometimes frustrate us, but if our eyes are firmly fixed on Jesus, neither trials, nor burdens, nor frustrations can stop us. Instead, they only become spiritual mountains, bringing us closer and closer to our spiritual potential.

AND WHAT IS THAT SPIRITUAL POTENTIAL?

As all men are alike and yet every man different, so is our spiritual potential. It is the same for every man—yet in every man it is different. Paul describes that potential in Romans 8:29, "... *For those God foreknew he also predestined to be conformed to the likeness of his Son, that he might be the firstborn among many brothers ...*" Being 'conformed' to Jesus simply means: acting in accordance with; showing identity to; resembling; or corresponding to His likeness. According to this verse that is God's spiritual vision us—and our spiritual potential. Consequently, He set in motion practical steps to bring it about: 1) He sent Jesus to earth as a man to live out the life He wants us to be conformed to. 2) He sent His Spirit to indwell and help us do it. 3) He made us part of a spiritual family of believers who are responsible for teaching, encouraging, exhorting and ministering to one another as each strives to be conformed to Christ. 4) He left us a ready audience with Him through the power of prayer. 5) He has provided us with an intercessor, who understands our struggles, and is willing to plead our cause (Hebrews 7:25). 6) He has promised that He will work in every circumstance to bring about good for us (Romans 8:28). 7) And to tie all of this together God has left us His written will for our lives, and the recorded life of His Son, who walked across the pages of the gospels touching the lives of men, calling us to follow His footprints.

Footprint #1 – HIS LIFE

As we observe the life of Jesus in the gospels, we know that it is not in our nature to respond to people, situations and circumstances as He did. It is even a little frightening to realize that God plans for us to do so. But He does, because Paul said, we are ". . . *predestined to be conformed to the image of Jesus . . .*" (Romans 8:29). He did not say it would be nice if we could be like Jesus, or that God really hopes we can be like Jesus. He said we are 'predestined' to be like Jesus. Which seems like an impossible dream as we each consider our weaknesses. But it is not an impossible dream for God. That is why He inspired Paul to write, ". . . *Do not conform any longer to the pattern of this world, but be transformed by the renewing of your mind . . .*" (Romans 12:2). Then He opens the door to that transformation when He explains what the "renewed" mind is in Philippians 2:5 (KJV), ". . . *Let this mind be in you which was also in Christ Jesus . . .*" Paul is saying that as Christians we have a choice, we do not have to be like the world. We can be changed. We can be changed by putting on the mind (or attitudes) of Christ—who gave up His rights, emptied Himself, and obeyed unto death. As a result, God exalted Him. And if we arm ourselves with the same mind, He will exalt us too—to new spiritual heights. Amen and amen.

But "self" stubbornly stands in the way. However, chapter 2 teaches us what "self" is and how self can be transformed with the attitudes (or mind) of Christ—making the "renewed self" an exciting spiritual asset. For dealing with "the old self" is not only the beginning of being conformed to Jesus' image, it is the first step to reaching for our spiritual potential.

Footprint #2 – JESUS AND THE WORD

We often overlook the power of the Word and the urgency of the command, ". . . *Let the word dwell in you richly . . .*" But Jesus didn't. He realized the value of scripture even at the age of twelve. In Luke 2:41-52 we are told about a trip to Jerusalem with His parents. And when it was time to go home He had disappeared, in typical 12 year-old fashion. So He was accidentally left behind. But He had not disappeared to a swimming hole, nor to any other place most 12 year-olds frequent. Instead He had gone to a place of learning, *". . . they found him in the temple courts, sitting among the teachers, listening to them and asking them questions . . ."* Eighteen years later we see Him skillfully using His knowledge of God's Word during a battle with Satan. A battle which took place when Jesus was physically weak from hunger and thirst. A battle in which Christ faced man's three greatest temptations: 1) self-preservation (He was tempted with food following His 40-day fast) 2) pride (He was challenged to prove He was the Son of God), and 3) riches (He was tempted with all the riches and power the earth had to offer). Which He resisted by focusing on 3 of God's teachings: 1) *". . . Man does not live on bread alone, but on every word that comes from the mouth of God . . ."* 2) *". . . Do not put the Lord your God to the test . . ."* 3) *". . . Away from me, Satan! . . . Worship the Lord your God, and serve him only . . ."*

Surprisingly, He did not use any of the powers we associate with His divinity in His struggle with Satan. What He used was scripture—the very same weapon God has given all of us (Ephesians 6:17). But this is not surprising when we consider: God's servants throughout time have relied on His inspired word. Paul emphasized, to his young brother Timothy, the impact it can have on your life when he wrote, *". . . All scripture is God-breathed and is useful for teaching, rebuking, correcting and training in righteousness, so that the man of God may be thoroughly equipped for every good work"* (2 Timothy 3:16,17). He also exhorted Timothy, *". . . Do your best to present yourself to God as one approved, a workman who does not need to be ashamed and who correctly handles the word of truth . . ."* (2 Timothy 2:15). David, also spoke of what God's teachings had meant in his life. Particularly, in Psalm 119:81-104.

> *". . . If your law had not been my delight*
> *I would have perished in my affliction*
> *. . . I will not forget your precepts,*
> *for by them you have renewed my life.*
> *. . . Your commands make me wiser than my enemies*
> *. . . I have more insight than all my teachers,*
> *for I meditate on your statutes."*

And which of us will not quickly praise the power of God's word and agree fully with: Jesus' example, Paul's admonition, and David's practical application. But if it stops there—if we are not motivated to actually spend time in the word—then it is only lip service—empty lip service at that. Just as empty as our spiritual growth will be. For if we are not feeding on the Word of Life, then we are vainly trying to exist on earthly bread alone. The result is: spiritual malnutrition.

Chapter 3 of this book teaches us how to: Recognize and Treat Spiritual Malnutrition in our lives. And how to let ". . . the Word dwell in us richly . . ." as we follow Jesus on to our Spiritual Potential.

Footprint #3 – JESUS AND PRAYER

You cannot follow the footprints of Jesus very far into the gospels or listen to His teachings very long without discovering the priority He placed on prayer. He did not treat prayer as just a 'nice, sweet' thing to do that made Him feel better. Instead we see Him treating it as a source of power. Because: 1) He was never too busy for prayer—On one occasion He missed a boat because He went off to the hills to pray (Matthew 14:23,24). 2) It was never too late for Him to pray—On occasions He prayed all night (Luke 6:12). 3) It was never too early for prayer—He got up before daylight to pray (Mark 1:35). 4) Prayer was a frequent part of His life—". . . But Jesus often withdrew to lonely places and prayed . . ." (Luke 5:16). 5) He prayed before making decisions—". . . and spent the night praying to God. When morning came, he called his disciples to him and chose 12 of them . . ." (Luke 6:12,13). 6) He prayed for others—". . . But I have prayed for you, Simon, that your faith may not fail . . ." (Luke 22:32). 7) He prayed for Himself—". . . Father, if you are willing take this cup from me; . . ." (Luke 22:41). 8) And He taught His followers about prayer (Matthew 6:5-9). If this man, who was the Son of God, the living Word, the Way, the Truth, and the Life, depended so much on prayer, how can we attempt to follow Him with a feeble, inconsistent prayer life? That isn't the prayer ministry He plans for us. For He taught that when we pray in accordance with God's will, the power of prayer is limitless in our lives, ". . . ask, and it shall be given you; seek, and ye shall find; knock, and it shall be opened unto you . . ." (Luke 11:9). Yet, our prayer lives are often empty and frustrating. Is that because prayer has lost its power? No, the problem is not with prayer the problem is with us.

Chapter 4 discusses the four major barriers to a strong prayer ministry, teaching us how to overcome them. As a result prayer can become a powerful force in our lives lifting us upward to our spiritual potential.

Footprint #4 — HIS MINISTRY

Jesus' footprints always led straight ahead, they never swerved, got side-tracked or bogged down. This was the result of knowing His purpose and clearly understanding His ministry (which is simply the work God gave Him to do). But without the right attitude toward that "work," His mission would have been a failure. Fortunately for us it wasn't. Also, to our good fortune, His attitude toward His ministry was recorded and left for us to see and imitate: 1) It was the most important thing in life to Him—". . . *My food . . . is to do the will of him who sent me and to finish his work . . .*" (John 4:34). 2) He treated it with urgency—". . . *As long as it is day, we must do the work of him who sent me. Night is coming, when no one can work . . .*" (John 9:4). 3) He did what needed to be done, whether He wanted to or not—". . . *Now my heart is troubled, and what shall I say? 'Father, save me from this hour'? No, it was for this very reason I came . . .*" (John 12:27). 4) He submitted to God's decisions in His ministry—". . . *For I have come down from heaven not to do my will but to do the will of him who sent me . . .*" (John 6:38). 5) And He completed His assignments—". . . *I have brought you glory on earth by completing the work you gave me to do . . .*" (John 17:4). No doubt, each of us longs to say to God at the end of our lives, ". . . *I have brought you glory on earth by completing the work you gave me to do.*" But very few of us feel that confident about our work for the Lord. Instead we usually feel God has a ministry for us but we are not sure we've found it yet. So we struggle with vague feelings of guilt, wanting to do more, wanting to be more effective, yet not knowing how.

Chapter 5 is designed to teach us how to be more effective through discovering our talents and our ministry. So we can confidently read, ". . . *For we are God's workmanship, created in Christ Jesus to do good works, which God prepared in advance for us to do . . .*" (Ephesians 2:10). And be free of vague feelings of doubt and guilt, eagerly looking forward to our ministry and spiritual potential.

Footprint #5 — LOVE AS JESUS LOVED

When Jesus said in John 13:34,35, ". . . *A new commandment I give you: Love one another. As I have loved you, so you must love one another. All men will know that you are my disciples if you love one another . . .*" He had a lot more in mind than just being "nice" to one another. This command was to be an integral part of God's plan to lead us and others to our spiritual potential. It is a multifaceted blessing. It enriches the life of the loved, the 'lovee' and the world that watches. For we cannot imitate Jesus love without:

1) being honest with ourselves and others,
2) being challenged to overcome pride, prejudice, selfishness and other sinful attitudes,
3) putting others' interests above our own, and
4) being identified as a disciple of Christ.

These are a few of the ways in which the "lovee" benefits. But the loved are also blessed:

1) they see a living testimony of Jesus life;
2) they are encouraged, edified, strengthened, supported, and lifted up;
3) they can be secure in this kind of love because it is not based on moods, looks, money, prestige, power, popularity, or any other temporary thing of the world.

But the watching world also benefits when we love one another:

1) they see a vision of what life can be,
2) they see some practical advantages to following Jesus, and
3) they are taught the validity of Jesus in the most powerful way possible—real life.

As we consider the impact this kind of love has on the spiritual body and the world, it is no wonder that it is not an option—but a command. A command we cannot submit to unless we have listened, watched, and followed Jesus. Otherwise, the love we display toward one another will only be 'love' by the world's definition—not love as Jesus lived it.

Chapter 6 of this book observes the way He loved His disciples, and applies it in a practical way to our daily interaction with one another. For learning to love as Jesus did is a vital part of our spiritual growth. Unless it is an active part of our daily lives, it is impossible for us to be conformed to the image of Christ.

Footprint #6 — JESUS AND THE SPIRIT

To neglect or ignore the function and power of the Spirit in the life of Jesus and the life of Christians would leave us literally blind to one of the most exciting and powerful dimensions of our Christian walk. For the one-on-one relationship of the Spirit and the Christian was part of the mystery that had been hidden through the ages. And was revealed only through Jesus and His teachings (Colossians 1:26,27).

The impact of the Spirit on the life of Christ is clearly displayed in the gospels. Notice, John the Baptist was to be filled with the Spirit from his birth (Luke 1:15). But no such statement is made concerning Jesus. Instead, we are told He was conceived by the Spirit but no further mention is made of the Spirit in Him until the time of His baptism. On that event, He came to John and asked to be baptized, "... to fulfill all righteousness ..." (Matthew 3:15). And as He came up out of the waters of baptism, the Spirit descended on Him in the bodily form of a dove, and the Father publicly acknowledged His Sonship, "... This is my Son, whom I love; with him I am well pleased ..." (Matthew 3:16,17; Luke 3:21,22). However, before this occasion, we know He was a remarkable young man. Because 18 years before, His grasp and insight of scripture was so profound the teachers of the Law in Jerusalem were amazed (Luke 2:47). But a study of Luke 4:13-44 details a noticeable difference in Him after the Spirit descended on Him. Remember, He had been living in Nazareth of Galilee for 30 years and no doubt had been reading the scripture in the synagogue since He was 18 (the normal age a Jewish boy started reading and speaking in synagogue).

Jesus could not have been the Christ without the power of the Spirit in His life. For it was the Spirit who:

1) conceived Him (Matthew 1:18; Luke 1:35)
2) empowered:
     His teachings (Luke 2:18,21)
     His ability to perform miracles (Matthew 12:27,28)
     to offer Himself as a sacrifice without blemish

If we belong to Jesus we are promised the Spirit will live "within" us (John 7:38; Acts 2:38; 5:32; Romans 8:9) benefiting and serving us and empowering us to live out the life Paul prayed for the Ephesians and us in Ephesians 3:14-21.

But, all too often, our Christian walk does not resemble Paul's prayer. Instead it is confused and feeble because we do not understand the power of the Spirit in our lives. Or it is arrogant and self-righteous because we misunderstand the role of the Spirit and His power.

Chapter 7 discusses: 1) what the Spirit does for the Christian, 2) the role He plays in our walk and growth, 3) spirituality and its effect on our lives, 4) sowing to the Spirit, and 5) keeping in step with the Spirit. The object of which is understanding and confidence of the Spirit's power and influence as we reach for our spiritual potential.

13

Chapter Two
Dealing With Self

Part 1
MY MIND

As we reach for our spiritual potential, the one person that will constantly be in our way is SELF. Self will be easily recognized for he will either be belligerent and stubborn or discouraged and defeated. And until we deal with SELF, following Jesus will be a pathway of constant conflict.

Since SELF lurks deep within us, it is often difficult to know where to begin to confront him. For he obscures his presence and identity with long, philosophical discussions, and unproductive hours of self-centeredness. But when we really get serious and take him in hand, we will discover Self is simply "Me" or:

(1) My Mind,
(2) My Behaviors, and
(3) My Emotions.

RENEWING OUR MIND

Paul gives us the first clue to dealing with self by teaching in Romans 12:2, ". . . *Do not conform any longer to the pattern of this world, but be transformed by the RENEWING OF YOUR MIND* . . ." He is saying, we can be changed, we can be different, and the key is in the renewed mind. But how do we "renew" our minds?

The first step is understanding what a "renewed" mind is. The second is learning how to develop it, and the third is prayerfully asking for God's help, strength, wisdom and power.

15

THE RENEWED MIND

It does not take a sincere Christian very long to realize that having a "renewed" mind is having the mind of Christ. In fact, Paul tells us in Philippians 2:5, ". . . let this mind be in you that was also in Christ . . ." To do so would require training our thoughts to imitate His thinking, putting on the attitudes He put on and living by the priorities He lived by.

Because the tools that shape our minds are: (a) our thoughts, (b) our attitudes, and (c) our priorities. These were the tools that conformed our minds to the patterns of the world originally. And they are the tools that can conform our minds to the mind of Christ now.

TRAINING OUR THOUGHTS

To make any successful change requires being honest and realistic about our present condition. And a little serious listening will quickly tell us the condition of our thought life. Do our thoughts focus on gossip, rumors, criticism, slander, envy, jealousy, unresolved anger, or bitterness? Or do they dwell on dreams and schemes for power, wealth, fame. Or are they filled with thoughts of sex, lust, sinful fantasy? Or, perhaps, our thoughts are a giant void of nothing, but apathy, complacency, or indifference.

But how can we think like Jesus? How can we even know His thoughts? Obviously, one way is by knowing His Words. For the words that we speak reflect our thinking. But Jesus said He spoke what He heard from God. However, John recorded some words spoken by Jesus in the 17th chapter that do reflect His thinking. They are words spoken from His heart to His Father in prayer.

JESUS THOUGHT ABOUT HIMSELF

In the first 5 verses of this chapter Jesus' thoughts focused on:
— the reality of His circumstance
— His purpose
— His power, authority
— the real meaning of eternal life
— the completion of His work for God
— where He came from and where He was going to

When we compare the emphasis of these thoughts to Philippians 4:8 (where Paul enumerates what our thoughts should dwell on), we can quickly see it coincides.

In these 5 verses Jesus thought about Himself yet He did not become self-centered. It is easy to become wrapped up in OUR needs, OUR wants, OUR weaknesses, OUR problems, etc., etc. And even though everything we are thinking about may be true and needed, if it becomes the total focus of our thinking, we tend to lose our purpose and direction for the Lord. What's more, we lose our perspective in life—because we see the rest of the world only through Me-Colored glasses.

JESUS THOUGHT ABOUT HIS DISCIPLES AND FUTURE BELIEVERS

John 17:5-26 reflects how others-oriented Jesus' thoughts were. Notice, of the 26 verses in this chapter, Jesus devoted only 5 to Himself. The rest of the prayer concerned others. For example, regarding His disciples he thought about:
— His responsibility to them
— their responsibility for their decisions
— where His opportunity to teach them came from
— whom He must return them to
— the glory they had already brought Him
— the glory they would bring Him in the future
— the future dangers they would face
— who could protect them in His absence
— their likeness to Him
— His commitment to them

His thoughts are remarkable when we consider that Jesus knew Judas would betray Him, Peter would deny Him, and all would desert Him. Even though His disciples had seen His miracles and heard His teachings for the past 3 years, they were still weak, worldly-minded and frustrating.

In Jesus place we would probably have thought, "Father, how can Judas do this to me, after all he has seen me do, and after all I have done for him. Even Peter, who has boasted he would follow me to the death, is going to deny me and then desert me with the rest. These men are so weak, what is going to happen to this world if this is the best it has to offer. I just don't see how this gospel business can possibly work out. We should probably be thinking about another plan."

But His thoughts concerning His disciples did not follow these lines. Instead He focused on what He could do for them, the glory they had brought him and God, and their acceptance of Him. In other words, He thought of them in a positive frame of mind with vision and appreciation.

This does not mean He did not face reality. He admitted His dis-

17

ciples would face divisive conflict, He admitted they would be hated because He was hated, and He admitted they would be in danger. He was also realistic about His ability to protect them, since He was returning to the Father.

But this confrontation with reality did not drive Him to worry, panic, or despair. It did drive Him to His Father—to ask God to protect His disciples. The result was His thoughts were free to continue His prayer for future believers and free to complete the mission He had been given.

GREAT THOUGHTS

A book of Wisdom in the Old Testament emphasizes the importance of our thoughts, Proverbs 23:7, ". . . As a man thinketh in his heart, so is he . . . ." This scripture is often used to support the world's definition of positive thinking (if I think I can do it, I can). But this interpretation is shallow, the scripture has much more depth. It is saying, the person we are began in our thoughts; in other words, we are becoming what we are thinking. Though no one can read our minds, anyone can know our thoughts if they wait and observe long enough—because our thoughts today will be our behavior on a future tomorrow.

So obviously, one of the quickest and surest ways to become great is to think great. And the quickest way to become Christ-like is to think Christ-like.

RENEWING YOUR ATTITUDE

There is probably not a kid in the United States that has not been told over and over, "You better straighten up your attitude." And probably very few actually knew what it meant—other than, "quit what you are doing and be nice about it."

Probably all of us have heard or even said, "They are just fantastic, they have the best attitude . . . or . . . I can't stand them, they have the worst attitude." And most of the time all we really mean is: we 'do' or 'do not' like them. The point is, the word 'attitude' is used and misused continuously in our culture without giving its meaning any serious thought.

Attitude is defined as: a mental approach or mental position to a fact. Does that help? Maybe this will: our thoughts are what we think, our attitude is the way we think.

For example, a positive attitude tends to see the best in every situation before it sees the worst. On the other hand, a negative attitude always sees what's wrong before it sees what's right. (And it rarely gets around to seeing anything 'right' because there is so much 'wrong' holding 'its' attention.)

A person with a negative attitude usually experiences a lot of conflict. They fight with the car dealer, the postman, the man down the street, the appliance repairman, the woman whose garbage can is spilling into the road, etc., etc. Their life is usually filled with long sessions of either: complaining, criticizing, telling someone off, or straightening someone out.

They rarely have a time they are free of worry, because something is always bothering them.

Can any of us picture Jesus living like that? We know He worked as a carpenter. And we know He lived in a village with other Jews. But, somehow we just don't see Him getting involved in situations where He would bicker with this person, complain about that person, tell this person off, straighten that person out. It just doesn't coincide with our image of Jesus.

Could it be that His attitude lifted Him above that way of life? Because the negative attitude is an attitude based on the patterns of the world (i.e., no one is going to take advantage of me). Patterns which Paul admonished us NOT to conform to. And the only way we can submit to that admonition is to conform to the attitudes of Christ. Or as Paul put it in, Ephesians 4:22, ". . . put off your old self, which is being corrupted by its deceitful desires; to be made new in the attitude of your minds . . ." And then he tells us how in Philippians 2:5-11, ". . . Your attitude should be the same as that of Christ Jesus:

> "Who, being in the very nature of God,
> did not consider equality with God
> something to be grasped,
> but made himself nothing,
> taking the very nature of a servant,
> being made in human likeness.
> And being found in appearance as a man,
> he humbled himself
> and became obedient to death—
> even the death on a cross!
> Therefore, God exalted him to the highest place
> and gave him the name that is above every name,
> that at the name of Jesus every knee should bow,
> in heaven and on earth and under the earth
> and every tongue confess that Jesus Christ is
> Lord, to the glory of God the Father."

19

Now what attitude does this passage display? Remember the definition of an attitude—a mental approach or position to a fact. And what were the facts:

FACT—Jesus was in the nature of God (with all the power and privileges involved [vs. 6, 7]).

JESUS' MENTAL APPROACH—He was 'willing' to give that up mentally (then later He gave it up physically).

FACT—Jesus became a man. (This statement is made so often it has lost much of its meaning for us. But one way to keep it in perspective is to realize that Jesus becoming a man is like a man agreeing to become a deer, or a bird, or a rabbit and live that life.)

JESUS' MENTAL APPROACH—He submitted to everything being a man involved. He endured ridicule, shame, humiliation, untrue accusations, beatings, even death. All administered by men that had no power to hurt Him unless He allowed it. And they didn't even realize "He was allowing it."

FACT—He was given meager physical resources to work with: a birth clouded with disgrace, a lowly background, the humble trade of a craftsman, minimal education, and no property. It might be compared to the owner of a Rolls Royce having to travel on a stick horse.

JESUS' MENTAL APPROACH—He thanked God for His daily bread. He did what He could with what He had and relied on God to make up the difference.

Three characteristics stand out as we consider the attitudes displayed in this passage: (a) selflessness, (b) *spiritual meekness, and (c) gratitude/appreciation.

Now what are the facts in our lives? What is our mental approach to them? For example:

FACT—I have the power of choice in a multitude of life situations.

MY MENTAL APPROACH—Do I deal with my choices based on what I want, like, deserve, have the right to OR do I base my choices on what is best for all concerned?

FACT—I am a woman/man.

MY MENTAL APPROACH—Do I resent what that involves? Do I rebel against all that state requires (jobs, child rearing, yard work, laundry, cooking, supporting a family, etc., etc.)?

FACT—I have a certain amount of wealth and health, etc. at my disposal.

---

* Spiritual meekness means whatever God does with my life is alright with me.

MY MENTAL APPROACH—Am I grateful for what I have been given or am I envious and resentful because others have more (forgetting that others also have less)?

As we compare our attitudes to those of Jesus we can probably see areas that need to change. But how do we change an attitude? We begin by changing our priorities.

RENEWING OUR PRIORITIES

At first glance, it may not seem appropriate to consider priorities a part of our mind. But for the purposes of this study, they must be included. Because our priorities influence our attitudes and our thoughts. And all three influence our decisions.

We could carry on a lengthy discussion about which has the greater impact on our decisions but it would be about as beneficial as 'which came first the chicken or the egg.' What is beneficial though is to realize that to develop a renewed mind requires developing renewed priorities—the priorities of Jesus.

There are a multitude of statements in the New Testament that reflect Jesus' priorities, but no more conclusive or dramatic than the statement spoken by Jesus in the Garden, ". . . Not my will but thy will be done . . ." This is more than a lovely thought and noble statement. It displays Jesus': submissiveness to God's will, His obedience to God, His trust in God, and His willingness to let God make the choice (even when He may not like it).

Each of these postures were the result of His priorities. And His priority was to do God's will. That was the basis of His "sinless" life.

This coincides perfectly with our mental image of Jesus. Because we visualize Him always WANTING to do things God's way. But Hebrews 5:7 says, ". . . he learned obedience by what he suffered . . ." So, He didn't always WANT to do things God's way. Sometimes He WANTED to do something different—just like us.

But we see Him taking a stand at the beginning of His ministry that made it possible for Him to do God's will even when He didn't want to. He established clearly defined priorities.

The first time we are introduced to His priorities is in the wilderness in open confrontation with Satan. And in that battle Jesus verbalized His priorities:

1) Serving God is more important than physical food.
2) Serving God is more important than the riches, power, glories, and pleasures of this world.
3) Serving God is more important than proving yourself.

Notice every temptation known falls into one of these categories—but the biggest temptation isn't stated. But it is very vividly portrayed.

21

And that is to let Satan upset or distort our priorities. And Satan is very effectively using the same strategy with us today. For any time Satan can upset our priorities, he has the biggest half of the battle won. But Jesus did not succumb to the temptations nor was He deceived—He had clearly defined His priorities and was committed to them.

Clearly defined priorities also protect us from a great deal of uncertainty and conflict when "it's"time to make decisions. In fact, established priorities actually eliminate many decisions, for example:

Early in our marriage, my husband and I decided that serving Jesus would be our first priority. So, we never really had to decide about church attendance. Our priority decided it for us. As our children were growing up they knew that we all went to church Sunday morning, Sunday night and Midweek Bible Study. The only time anyone did not go to church was when they were sick. Then the rest of the family went. They never had to ask (or argue), "Are we going to church today? . . . Do we have to go to church?" The priority was set and the decision was made, and complaining did as much good as complaining about going to school.

I know families that every church service is an issue. Are we are aren't we, can we or can't we, will we or won't we? And the evidence of such unclear priorities is very evident.

We never had to decide on divorce because we were BOTH committed to God's Word and His teachings on marriage. If we had a problem, we settled it God's way. Since we were not going to get a divorce, we had no other choice.

When I work with someone coming out of the world into the life of Jesus, the first thing I have them do is define their priorities. Then, I have them sit down and go over their old lifestyle and see how it fits their new priorities. They eliminate the things that will not conform and alter the pattern of things that are questionable.

Consequently, they avoid so much temptation, conflict and, often times, sin. For example, if they quit buying liquor and going to bars, they don't have to decide whether or not to get drunk.

THE CONCLUSION

From Jesus' answers to Satan, we can tell He had studied the scriptures (as had every Jewish boy) and had already made His decisions before He confronted Satan. Then when temptation came, He really did not have to struggle with a decision, it had already been made.

See the possibility for victory. As we study God's Word, we can make our decisions, establish our priorities, and then when Satan tempts us, we can say confidently with Jesus, "Get thee behind me Satan."

DISCUSSION QUESTIONS

1. What point in the section on our 'thoughts' had the most impact on you? Why?
2. What point in the section on 'attitudes' had the most impact on you? Why?
3. What point in the section on 'priorities' had the most impact on you? Why?
4. How does Matthew 22:37 compare to this overall chapter?
5. How does Romans 1:28 relate to this chapter?

Dealing With Self

Part 2
MY BEHAVIOR

In our current culture there is so much emphasis on attitudes and motives, we have almost lost sight of the importance of behavior. Although attitudes and motives count, so does behavior.

We can be assured of this by the multitude of commands in the Word. Some Christians are fond of saying the Old Law was a law of rules and commands, but the New Covenant is a Covenant of grace without rules or commands. That concept is a fantasy. The New Covenant is a Covenant of Grace, but there are over 500 direct commands listed in the New Testament. And a multitude of those commands focus on our behaviors.

From looking at them, we can see they break down into two separate categories: (a) commands that train us in righteous behavior, (b) commands that protect us from Satan's snares.

COMMANDED BEHAVIORS THAT TRAIN

A very good example of commands designed to train us in righteous behaviors is listed in Ephesians 4:22-32. We won't go over them individually, but let's look at the principle involved. And that principle is; replace wrong behaviors with right behaviors (behavior modification).

The drawing below illustrates the steps that lead up to making the behavior decision. And the consequences that follow that decision.

As we travel life's path we constantly approach life's EVENTS (ballgames, shopping trips, dental appointments, job situations, etc.). And as we approach those events we view them from OUR perspective. (Our perspective consists of our thoughts, attitudes, and priorities.)

Next, we enter the actual event and as a result we experience EMOTIONS; following which, we decide on some kind of behavior response. Depending on that decision, we either circle up into God's abundant life or we drop down into the way of the natural man.

Now let's impose a life situation on this model—You are taking a leisurely stroll around the neighborhood. All of a sudden 2 kids come tearing out of an alley on their bicycles. They almost run over you, scaring you to death, forcing you to leap out of the way—after sur-

24

viving the initial shock, angry feelings start exploding. Now you are at the junction and it is decision time. What are you going to do about your angry feelings? (Or, what is your behavioral response going to be?) As you stand at this crossroad you can turn the way of your sinful man or you can travel in the way of God's teachings.

The sinful man's way:

(1) You can chase the kids down the street yelling curses, you can bang on their mother's door and threaten to have her kids arrested or sued or both, you can try to sick your dog on them the next time they ride by your house, or

God's way:

(2) you can overlook the incident just making a note to watch for them in the future, or you can speak the truth in love telling them about the dangers involved.

In the first response you circled down into sinful behavior patterns that are filled with guilt, conflict, anger, resentment, etc. And with this response you reinforced that pattern in your life. In other words, exploding makes it just that much easier to explode the next time. Because behavioral responses are habit forming.

In the second response you circled up into the peace, freedom from conflict, freedom from guilt, the comfort of a clear conscience, etc. All of which are features of the abundant life. And with this response you have reinforced this pattern in your life. Because 'good' behavioral responses are just as habit forming as 'bad' ones.

COMMANDED BEHAVIORS THAT PROTECT

We all have our children's best interest at heart when we tell them not to touch a stove, play with a knife, run with a pencil. We love them and don't want them to suffer the consequences we know are possible.

God has the same motives when He forbids us to be involved in certain behaviors. He knows the consequences. He knows that not only will the behavior endanger us with an earthly consequence; but the disobedience to Him will also have a future consequence. For example:

. . . do not steal . . .

There is a danger we will get caught and go to prison. Stealing reinforces selfishness on our part—because we are taking for ourselves what belongs to someone else. Both of these will cause us conflict on earth—and if unrepented of, they will have a consequence in eternity.

. . . do not be sexually immoral . . .

There is danger to our physical bodies through disease. An unwanted child could possibly be conceived. Hearts can be broken because of the intimacy of the relationship without protection of the

25

serious commitment of marriage. All of these sins can be forgiven but many of the consequences have to be lived out.

. . . do not lie, rage, slander . . .

All of these sinful behaviors include conflict, deceit, and pain. They can all be forgiven. But in many cases, people are hurt and will bear the scars of those wounds for years.

THE THREE-FOLD PURPOSE OF OBEDIENCE

Obeying God's commands does train us in righteous behavior and they protect us and those are reasons enough for us to obey. But there is an additional reason to obey God's commands that brings glory to God, His Son and His Word. And that purpose is disclosed in the following verses.

GLORY TO GOD

Listen to Jesus in John 14:31, ". . . *but the world must learn that I love the Father and that I do exactly what my Father has commanded me . . .*" This is Jesus Christ the Son of God. He had lived a perfect life and glorified God in many ways, yet He said that the world must learn He LOVED God. And the way He displayed this love was by doing exactly what God said.

GLORY TO JESUS

And Jesus also said, ". . . *All men will know that you are my disciples if you love one another . . .*" (John 14:35). Jesus had told them to 'love one another.' Now He tells them their obedience to this command will bring glory to Him. He prays for this same thing in John 17.

GLORY TO THE WORD

And Paul added, ". . . *to be self-controlled and pure, to be busy at home, to be kind, and to be subject to their husbands, so that no one will malign the Word of God . . .*" Again, we see how much impact our obedience has on the way the world views God, His Son and His Word.

DISCUSSION QUESTIONS

1. What point in Part 2 had the most impact on you? Why?
2. Discuss John 14:31 in relation to this section.
3. Discuss 1 Peter 2:13-16 in relation to this section.
4. How does James 4:7 compare to the behavior diagram in this section? (Remember fear is a feeling.)

26

Dealing With Self

Part 3
MY EMOTIONS

Emotions are simply our feelings and our present culture is FEEL-ING oriented. Feelings are good—they are a gift to mankind that serves and enhances his life in a variety of ways.

But our present culture has almost made our feelings our God. And as a result "feelings" have become the basis of many of our values and decisions, i.e., "if it feels good, do it."

This is NOT what the Bible teaches. Listen to 1 Peter 3:6, ". . . *do what is right and do not give way to fear . . .*" Fear is a feeling. But Peter said to base your behavior on what is RIGHT not on fear.

Then in 2 Timothy 4:5, ". . . *But you keep your head in all situations . . .*" In this passage Paul is telling Timothy that no matter what anyone else does, he must keep his head. In other words, react in logic based on knowledge and wisdom.

Christ left an example in John 12:27, ". . . *Now my heart is troubled, and what shall I say? Father save me from this hour? No, it was for this very reason I came to this hour. Father glorify your name.*"

In this passage we see Jesus dealing with His emotions:
—He acknowledged them (my heart is troubled)
—He verbalized this option (should I say . . . save me . . .)
—He made a decision (No, it was for this very reason . . .)
—and He was strengthened.

A similar model to the one on behavior can be used. We approach an event seeing it from our perspective (our thoughts, attitudes, priorities). We experience the event, we experience the feelings, then we face our options (deal with it God's way or sin's way). Then we decide on our behavioral response.

But many people never go through the decision making process. Because the patterns of past behaviors are so strong their responses are automatic. Take, for instance, the high tempered person that has a pattern of responding to angry feelings through explosions. They probably aren't aware they have a choice, the other is so automatic—besides it feels good.

But we do have a choice, otherwise, how could the scriptures in Ephesians 4:22-5:21; 1 Peter 3:6; 2 Timothy 4:5 be valid. But to overcome sinful responses to feelings (angry, sexual, fearful, etc.), we must learn and live discipline until God's patterns are established in

27

our lives. Because a life based on God's teachings and facts may have some ups and downs but they are on a plane that is gradually sloping upward to new spiritual heights.

While a life based only on feelings has its ups and downs and never goes anywhere.

So if we would reach to fulfill God's vision for us we must take Paul's admonition to heart and keep our heads in all situations so we can develop God's patterns in our lives as we reach for our spiritual potential.

DISCUSSION QUESTIONS

1. What point in Part 3 had the most impact on you? Why?

2. Discuss Philippians 4:12 in relation to this section. Focus on the phrase, 'learned to be content.'

3. Discuss Colossians 3:2 in relation to this section. Is "affection" a feeling? How can you set it on things above?

4. Can you implement Ephesians 5:15 based on feelings alone? Explain your answer.

Chapter Three

Recognize and Treat Spiritual Malnutrition

Spiritual malnutrition is one of the major obstacles for spiritual growth in our day and time. And alarmingly, it has reached epidemic proportions among church members throughout the country. Its symptoms are many and can be experienced in part, in total, or in a variety of combinations, with the most common appearing to be: discouragement, frustration, the feeling of being separated from brethren and God, irregular church attendance, low resistance to sin, a hesitant faith, uncertainty of salvation, disassociated feelings of guilt, the impression that God is not quite pleased with you, etc., etc. Needless to say, it is impossible to live the abundant life described in the New Testament while suffering from the symptoms of Spiritual Malnutrition. So recognizing and treating it is a MUST, but to do so requires: (1) being familiar with its symptoms, (2) understanding its root cause, and (3) conscientiously applying the solution; all of which are easier when we compare it to its physical counterpart—physical malnutrition.

GOD'S SCHEME IN CREATION

The world was created by God and continues on his master scheme; and that scheme functions through the use of natural laws, i.e., the law of gravity. Though we can't physically see the law of gravity, we know it exists from observing its effect: for example, the certainty of falling if we step off the roof of a building. Another natural law God utilized in His order of creation could be paraphrased: every living organism must have a source of energy. In other words, everything must be fed. This law cannot be seen either, but we can certainly see its effect. Ignoring it, either by choice, ignorance or deprivation will result in physical malnutrition just as surely as stepping off a building will result in falling. By the same token, God has created spiritual laws that are just as certain as natural laws. With this in mind, let's compare the feeding and growth of the physical and spiritual man from infancy to adulthood.

It's amazing how similar the physical and spiritual man are. For example: both experience birth, both are subject to growth, both can know death, both are capable of strength and weakness, both live a life of struggle, and both require a source of energy (food).

THE PHYSICAL INFANT

The feeding program for the PHYSICAL INFANT must consist of: (1) Regularity—A newborn may require 24 ozs. of milk in a 24 hour period (approximately 15 to 20% of its body weight). Its growth and development are more rapid than at any other time of life. But it cannot take 24 ozs. at one time and wait another 24 hours to eat again. The infant would expel what it could not hold, then wail in hunger until the next feeding. So, nature guaranteed the meeting of this need by: causing the newborn discomfort when it needs food . . . which causes the newborn to wail . . . which causes the mother to jump and feed the baby—regularly. (2) Frequency—an infant requires a large amount of food yet the stomach capacity is small. Therefore, the feeding must not only be regular it must also be frequent (even day and night at the beginning). (3) Appropriate Food—Beefsteak is excellent food for an adult but not for an infant. The newborn does not have the physical tools (teeth) to ingest it nor the digestive tract to assimilate and utilize it. (4) Assistance—An infant is incapable of meeting its own nutritional requirements. It does not have the knowledge or the physical skills. If it is to survive, it must have someone's attention and care.

THE EFFECT

If these needs are met (barring other problems), the infant will develop and grow. It will have good coloring, appropriate skills for its age, be curious and interested, eager to learn, have good general health, be resistant to disease, and happy. If these needs are NOT met, the infant's physical and mental growth will be impaired. It will alternate between listlessness and irritability, it will be slow in developing skills, have a low resistance to disease and experience poor general health.

Infancy is a CRITICAL period, for there is little reserve strength and energy to meet the needs of physical trauma or crisis.

THE SPIRITUAL INFANT

The feeding needs of the spiritual infant are remarkably like those of the physical infant. It must be fed: (1) Regularly—a spiritual infant thrives on regular feedings. It would benefit very little from a marathon reading of the whole Bible (a spiritual food) over a 5 day period. Most of the information would be lost because the physical mind would be incapable of retaining it and the spiritual mind would be too immature to utilize it. Instead, it needs a consistent flow of energy all the time, which is obtained through regularly partaking of spiritual food. (2) Frequently—because the spiritual infant is also growing and changing very rapidly, its energy needs far exceed its storage capacity (memory banks). Therefore, it requires regular and frequent feedings to meet its rapid growth potential. (3) Appropriate Food—a spiritual infant needs spiritual food it can assimilate. Peter refers to it in 1 Peter 2:2,3 and Paul also mentions the appropriateness of different types of spiritual food for different levels of spiritual maturity in 1 Corinthians 3:1-3. Spiritual infants often excitedly leap into a study of prophecy and Revelation only to become confused and discouraged; a predictable result, when we realize they do not have the spiritual teeth to ingest it, nor the spiritual maturity to assimilate and utilize it. (4) Assistance— God left the physical infant's survival totally dependent on human beings. But, wisely, He did not leave the spiritual infant in that position. He gave the newborn the Holy Spirit (Acts 2:42; Romans 8:27) which can intercede on his behalf, even if abandoned by his spiritual family. But God does not intend the spiritual infant to be deserted. For just as He provided for the care of the newborn physical baby through the home, He left provision for the care of the newborn spiritual baby through the church.

THE EFFECT

If these needs ARE met (barring other spiritual problems) the newborn will thrive. It will grow and be spiritually healthy, happy, involved, excited about its faith, resistant to sin, and confident in its salvation. If these needs are NOT met, its growth will be impaired. It will be spiritually: unhappy, uninvolved, easily discouraged, given to criticism and complaint, susceptible to disease, lack confidence in its salvation, and struggle with feelings of guilt. Spiritual infancy is also a CRITICAL period. The patterns of the abundant life are not yet established in its daily routines. It has minimal religious experience to draw from in the event of spiritual trauma or crises.

31

THE PHYSICAL OR SPIRITUAL CHILD

The child's (physical or spiritual) nutritional needs are very similar to those of the infant (physical or spiritual). However, there are a few differences.

The child can adopt a more adult feeding routine. It should be able to manage many of its feeding needs and can utilize foods that were beyond its capabilities as an infant.

If a child practices good nutrition (and barring other problems), the result will be comparable to those of the infant; continued growth and good general health, abundant energy, interested, involved, enthusiastic and excited, with a countenance that is "lifted up."

If its nutrition is poor, the effect will resemble those of the infant: impaired growth, poor general health, uninvolved, disinterested, listless, cross and irritable, susceptible to disease, and have a countenance that "has fallen."

THE PHYSICAL OR SPIRITUAL ADULT

A remarkable thing about our bodies: we never outgrow our need for food. By age 40, the average adult has eaten approximately 2 tons of food. But if that average adult quits eating entirely, in a very short time he will begin to experience physical symptoms warning him of his body's need for nutrition.

The feeding requirements for the adult (physical or spiritual) are not drastically different from those of the infant. The adult must continue to eat: regularly, frequently, and appropriately (according to his body's needs). However, he should be able to supervise his own diet, discipline himself to adhere to it, and assist with the care and feeding of others.

THE EFFECT ON THE PHYSICAL ADULT

The results of good physical nutrition on the physical adult (barring other physical problems) are: proper weight, better health, physical and mental energy, with a good overall countenance and sense of well being. Amazingly, the list of symptoms resulting from poor physical nutrition in the adult can be longer than for an infant or child. They are: improper blood sugar, headaches, fatigue, fainting spells, improper weight and its complications, withdrawal, indifference, lack of involvement, crossness and irritability, etc.

THE EFFECT ON THE SPIRITUAL ADULT

The results of good spiritual nutrition (barring other spiritual problems) are: confidence in our salvation, love for the family of God, joy in our relationship with Christ, a sense of peace and purpose, a faith that motivates, and abundant enthusiasm.

The result of poor spiritual nutrition also exceeds those of the child or infant. They are: uncertainty of salvation, the feeling of isolation from brethren, uncomfortableness in fellowship, vague feelings of guilt, indifference and lack of involvement, etc.

NOW WHAT?

SYMPTOMS ARE MERELY WARNINGS

It is encouraging to know the symptoms of spiritual malnutrition in our lives, can be reversed. For malnutrition (physical or spiritual) does not kill quickly. Its symptoms are warning signs that something is amiss in our lives. And when they appear, we are faced with a choice: (1) we are going to heed the warnings and make the necessary changes to correct our problem, or (2) we are not. If we choose to alter our nutrition program, three tools will be required: determination, commitment and planning. If we choose to ignore the warnings, we can expect them to become more severe until we lapse into a coma, which eventually leads to death. And though the spiritual coma is a very dangerous condition, it's victim is usually unaware of his/her condition while the victim of "near starvation" truly continues to suffer, eating just enough to stay alive but not enough to be healthy, feel good and experience any of the joys of living. A phrase has been coined that perfectly describes this state when it afflicts the spiritual man: "Just enough religion to make him miserable."

GOD HAS PREPARED A FEAST

But God did not intend for man to live a miserable existence. He provided an abundant feast for His creation both physical and spiritual. The feast He created to nurture the spiritual man consists of: prayer, fellowship, love, evangelism, obedience, and time in the Word. And for good spiritual health and growth a Christian must partake of ALL, but the staff of this feast is Time in The Word. The Word is the basis of our life in Christ according to Matthew 4:4. When we neglect it, even the other spiritual foods become weak and ineffective. Then symptoms of spiritual malnutrition soon appear in our hearts and in our lives, creating a condition that only the Word can cure.

A SPIRITUAL SELF-EXAMINATION

The medical fields emphasize continually the importance of medical check-ups. They stress the urgency of catching life threatening conditions while they can still be cured. Yet our physical bodies last only a few years. If it is urgent we get check-ups to protect what lasts only a few years at best, how much more urgent would a check-up be for the body that will live forever.

As we considered the symptoms of spiritual malnutrition, many of us may have recognized some of the symptoms in our own lives. If we did not compare them to our lives, we can ask ourselves one diagnostic question and immediately know if we need to be better nourished spiritually, "Do I think God is pleased with my spiritual growth?" Most of us would probably answer that question with an, "I doubt it." The "I doubt it" answer or any version thereof indicates one of two things: (1) that we need to alter our spiritual nutrition program because we are malnourished, or (2) we need to alter our nutrition program because we are not confident of our relationship with God.

HOW MUCH AND HOW OFTEN?

Anytime we commit ourselves to spending time in The Word, the first question that comes to mind is "how much and how often?" There is NO exact rule, just as there is no exact rule for physical feedings. But the perimeters for both are individual need and convenience. To determine individual nutritional need, we must examine our spiritual man. Are we pleased with his growth and fitness? If so, then we need to continue with our nutritional program. If we are not satisfied, we need to make some changes. We'll find that as our spiritual nutrition improves, so does our: peace of mind, Christian fellowship, confidence in our salvation, and our daily responses to life situations. After an honest examination, few Christians rarely conclude they DO NOT NEED to feed on God's Word, and most will admit they need it daily. But there are a variety of reasons why we don't, for example: (1) We know we should, but when the time comes, we don't have the desire and we would feel like a hypocrite doing it, (2) We know we should, but we just can't find the time in our schedule, (3) We've really tried but we just don't know what to read, or (4) We've tried several times, but we just don't get anything out of it. The most fortunate thing about all of these reasons, is that with determination and God's help, they can be overcome.

WHEN WE KNOW WE SHOULD,
BUT WE HAVE NO DESIRE

If we have decided to spend time in the Word daily, yet at the chosen time we have no desire—spend time anyway. Feeding on the Word when we don't want to is not hypocrisy, it's good discipline! Our culture has mishandled the word hypocrisy. It has come to mean: doing what we don't want to do, which is not hypocrisy. Hypocrisy is living a lie. It is giving the impression we live one way when in fact we live another. The difference between discipline and hypocrisy can be seen more clearly when we compare it to caring for a baby. How many wet diapers have we really looked forward to changing—none? But we changed them anyway. Does that make us hypocrites? No, it makes us good parents. By the same token, spending time in the Word on the days we are looking forward to it and on the days we are not, doesn't make us hypocrites—it makes us disciplined, committed, and better nourished Christians. In addition, it is exciting to discover that we can develop a craving for the Word. A craving that makes the days we are reluctant to open the Bible fewer and fewer. We develop this "craving for" by simply "partaking of." Think about it. How did we learn to "want" the foods we like; by eating them. Appetites are trained. David recognized this when he said in Psalm 119, ". . . I meditate on your statutes and I delight in them . . . I meditate on your teachings and I rejoice . . ." Notice, first he meditated THEN he delighted and rejoiced.

WHEN WE CAN'T WORK IT INTO OUR BUSY SCHEDULE

The only way to work it in is by: WORKING IT IN. And the first step is the decision to do so. After we make that decision, we must not fall into the trap of RE-MAKING it every day. Anytime we get up and ask ourselves if we are going to spend time in the Word, there's a 99% chance we won't. It's the same as asking ourselves if we are going to church today. Within 15 minutes we will be staying home. We will be too sick, too tired, too washed-out, or coming down with something. After we once make the decision to spend time in the Word daily—we should never question it again. It should be assumed just like our physical feeding time is assumed. Do we ever get out of bed and ask ourselves if we are going to eat? No, we know we are. All we ask ourselves is "when and what."

Next, work it in. We work in other necessary tasks based on: need, importance, personal preference, etc. We schedule them at practical, appropriate times for us. We must use the same wisdom, priority and ingenuity in scheduling our spiritual feeding time. However, after deciding, scheduling and spending regular time in the Word, if the plumbing erupts, the house burns and the Russians attack, let's not take a month long guilt trip. We occasionally miss physical meals too.

WHEN WE TRY
BUT DON'T KNOW WHAT TO READ

All food provides some source of energy for the physical man and any contact with the Word will benefit the spiritual man. However, that benefit will be much greater if we make sure our spiritual needs are being met by: (1) Planning our spiritual menu. (2) Not settling for the Bible "fall opens" (which is just spiritual pot luck). They are pleasant treats occasionally, but they cannot be depended on to meet all our nutritional requirements. (3) Analyzing our needs and using this time to meet them, i.e., if our faith is weak—we could look up every scripture in the concordance listed under faith; if our relationship with Christ is mediocre—we can feed on the Gospel of John followed with 1, 2 and 3 John; or if we are having difficulty applying our Christianity—we need to absorb the Book of James.

WHEN WE'VE TRIED
BUT DON'T GET ANYTHING OUT OF IT

Maybe we are "reading" instead of "feeding" and there is a decided difference. Simply reading the Word could be compared to going up and down the aisle of a supermarket memorizing every item on the shelf. It's beneficial for helping others find what they need or finding what we need in a hurry; but, unless we eat, we can starve to death in a supermarket. Feeding is ingesting the Word. Getting it inside of you so it can be used by the spiritual man, digesting and making it a part of you.

Just as reading and feeding are not one and the same, neither is "class preparation" and "feeding on the Word." Studying to teach a class is like cooking a feast for others. Too often we find ourselves so busy preparing for others, that we only have time to nibble around the edges or hurriedly eat while standing over the sink. We can spend hours and hours in Bible study and still suffer from many of the symptoms of spiritual malnutrition. (A trap that many ministers fall into.)

A PROGRAM FOR OVERCOMING
SPIRITUAL MALNUTRITION

The program listed below is not the only way to treat spiritual malnutrition. You may discover a method for treating it that is more workable for you. But, this program has been kitchen tested in my own spiritual kitchen and won the Doris Black "Good Spiritual Nutrition" Award. Therefore, if you don't have something better, why not

36

try mine until you get one worked out to meet your special needs. However, let me warn you, it is just like any other diet, it only works—when you use it. (1) Keep a Bible, a pen and a notebook in the same place—if you have to look for your tools, you will put it off till later (and later is like tomorrow, it never comes). Using the same place for your time in the Word is also valuable. Association plays an important part in your ability to focus your mind. Consider how your mind reacts when you enter a church, a football stadium, etc. So take advantage of your mind's association and partake of the Word regularly in the same place. (For example, I keep my tools on a stand by a comfortable chair in our bedroom. When I go to that corner in the morning, my mind automatically starts turning to times I have spent there before.) (2) Plan to spend only 15 to 20 minutes at your spiritual feast. You may spend more, but if you have committed to longer, you tend to put off starting, waiting until you have more time. So commit yourself to only 15 or 20 minutes, which you can always find. (3) When you study deeply (ingesting the Word), you probably cannot cover more than 2 or 3 verses a day.

I have discovered three levels of understanding in deep study and I am convinced it takes all three before the word becomes a part of you:

a) First, read the scripture, then write it down in your own words. In other words, paraphrase it.

b) Second, write down what that scripture is telling you, how it affects your life, behavior, attitudes, beliefs.

c) Third, wait a while longer and write down any additional insight. Writing the scripture and your thoughts down is an absolute MUST for deep Bible study. Yet, it is the step that Christians most often want to skip. Many Christians come to me years after I have urged using this method and excitedly tell of the growth they experienced after they finally started "writing out" the scriptures and their thoughts. It never surprises me, for I know the dynamic involved. The writing forces them to verbalize the concepts they are learning, it rules out vagueness and fuzzy thinking, it reinforces what they are learning and it provides research for future class preparation. Before I developed this spiritual feeding program, I had spent hundred of hours studying, reading and learning the Word. I knew what most of the commentaries said about most of the scriptures, and with my trusty concordance I could find most scriptures in the blink of an eye. I rarely read less than 10 chapters at one sitting. I had been through the Bible from front to back many, many times. Yet I suffered several of the symptoms of spiritual malnutrition. I kept feeling that God was not pleased with me. That there was something more He wanted of me—yet I could not see what. That feeling drove me in desperation to start "feeding" on the Word instead of just reading it, memorizing it and preparing it for others. First the symptoms I felt began to diminish and then disappeared entirely. Next, they were replaced with: certainty of my salvation, confidence in my relationship with God, enthusiasm in my faith, and excitement about His family (the Church). Now I can joyfully say with David, "I contemplate on your statutes and I delight in them." And I pray that God would say of me, "She is a servant after my own heart."

DISCUSSION QUESTIONS

1. What point in this lesson had the most impact on you? Why?
2. Have you ever experienced any of the symptoms of spiritual malnutrition?
3. Why did God leave the written Word?
4. How many Bibles do you have in your home? What kind of responsibility does that give you? Will you be relieved of any responsibility if you get rid of all your Bibles?
5. How can we implement Colossians 3:16?
6. How can we obey Ephesians 6:17?

Chapter Four
When the Problem With Prayer Is Me

Part 1
KNOW HOW TO PRAY

Have you ever struggled with a problem and were counseled by other Christians, "pray about it," your answer was, "I have," yet, you were still struggling? Have you ever taken your problems to the Lord and come away feeling guilty because you still felt burdened? Does it seem God never grants your prayer requests? Have you come to the conclusion that you must be asking "amiss" as spoken of in James 4:3. But you don't understand how for you are conscientiously trying to pray as God would have you to.

If you have experienced this dilemma in a major or a minor way, then the dimension for spiritual growth in prayer is especially for you. I particularly identify with you because I struggled with a weak prayer ministry for years until I did an in-depth study on prayer and discovered—How To Overcome The Four Major Barriers To A Powerful Prayer Ministry.

In this study I found that the main barrier for me had been my inability to see how God granted my prayer petitions. The next chapter will deal with that dimension of prayer exclusively, but the first three barriers (which we will be looking at in this chapter) have the potential to be just as great a handicap. They are: (1) lack of planning, (2) not knowing how to pray, and (3) not being specific. Surprisingly, as you improve any one of these areas the others improve proportionately.

39

OVERCOMING BARRIER #1 –
LACK OF PLANNING

Planning your prayer life sounds so structured and routine that it almost smacks of insincerity. But I believe that reaction is more the result of our own mental image of prayer than the result of information gleaned from the Word of God.

In the gospels, we see that Jesus took time to pray regularly. Much too regularly for it to be a hit-and-miss-whenever-He-could-find-the-time arrangement. He must have planned for time in prayer and then took that time in prayer for the scriptures to be able to mention so frequently, ". . . *Jesus went aside to pray* . . ."

But unfortunately, we often treat prayer as though it must be spontaneous to be sincere. And we will have many spontaneous occasions to pray—but if that is the only time we pray, our prayer life will be just about as consistent and successful as (1) our public worship would be if we worshipped only spontaneously, or, (2) as successful as our house or yard work would be if they were only taken care of when the mood struck us. Yet with our lives constantly bombarded by: jobs, car pools, meetings, homework sessions, cleaning, cooking, yard work, getting the car lubed, trips to the doctor, dentist, orthodontist, band practice, soccer games, Bible classes, etc., etc., there never seems an appropriate time to pray. And to add to the dilemma the things we are usually doing are important tasks that we can't and shouldn't neglect. But often times "doing good things" is one of Satan's most effective weapons against a devoted Christian. A person dedicated to the Lord is not going to fall for Satan's "Let's do something wicked instead of talk to God" routine. But dedicated people often get so involved doing the good things that there is very little time left for communing with God.

"But isn't doing good things what Christianity is all about?" Yes, and Jesus did the biggest and the best things of all. But, Christ returned to heaven while there were still people on the earth that needed to be healed, needed to be taught, needed to be ministered to. Even He did not finish off every "good deed," nor can we. But one thing Jesus did NOT leave undone was time in prayer, evidently. He needed it to do His Father's will—and if He did, we certainly do. On the other hand, if His time in prayer is mentioned so often just to leave the example for us, the conclusion is the same. We NEED time in prayer.

Note, many of the times ". . . *Jesus went aside to pray* . . ." He was in the midst of teaching, healing, etc. I do not believe this example teaches that we should stop in the middle of teaching, etc. and make a big ordeal of 'going aside to pray'; but, it certainly does teach Jesus placed a high priority on talking to His Father.

"But how do you go about finding time?" Unfortunately, you can never "find" time for prayer, you must "make" time for prayer and that takes PLANNING. The first step in any plan is a decision. The next step is to make that decision a commitment and the third step is to follow it through. This is a universal principle and a scriptural principle. In James 1:6-8 we are told, ". . . A person who doubts is like a wave blown and tossed—a person like that will not receive anything from God for he is unstable in all of his ways . . ." In that passage James is speaking of asking God for wisdom—but this is a "truth" that is applicable in all situations. An unstable person does not receive anything because he does not stick to a course. So if you want your prayer life to change into a faith-building ministry, make a decision that you are going to change your prayer life—make that decision a commitment—and follow it through.

MAKE A SPECIFIC PLAN

If you decide to improve your prayer life by praying more often, it will be just about as successful as deciding to diet more often. Neither will come to much. A plan for spending time in prayer must be just as specific as a plan for dieting. And with the type and variety of our responsibilities this is not easy—but it is possible.

MAKE A PRAYER CYCLE

We often dread starting prayer, because we have so many things to pray about. We know it is going to take us 30 to 40 minutes . . . and we don't have that much time right now . . . and we'll be exhausted by the time we finish . . . and we are expecting a phone call, and so we put it off until bedtime. But the next morning we do not awake feeling refreshed from our time in prayer, we awake feeling guilty because we fell asleep after praying for only the very top portion of our list. And we wonder what is wrong with our faith that we can't even stay awake long enough to place in God's hands our needs and the needs of others.

Let's use our heads. It doesn't take long to realize that to do everything in the whole house every day is impossible. So we develop a schedule to keep everything done without killing ourselves. Be just as smart in dealing with your prayer responsibilities. I use a prayer cycle: Monday I pray for our married children and their families; Tuesday I pray for our parents, brothers and sisters and other close relatives; Wednesday, I pray for brothers and sisters in Christ that I know have particular needs; Thursdays I pray for our church leaders, church programs, and our government leaders; Friday I pray for my husband and myself. That does not mean that I do not pray for these at other times—but my "thought out" concerns are taken care of regularly.

Do you know what a "thought out" concern is? A thought out concern is a request that you have taken time to seriously consider in someone's behalf. We frequently spend more time selecting the "right" birthday gift for someone we love than choosing a blessing for them from God's great wealth. Paul's writings give us some examples of specific "thought out" blessings he requested. For example, in Colossians 4:2-6, he asked the Colossians to pray to God to open a door for his message, and that he could proclaim it clearly. An example of a thought out concern for one of my prayer benefactors might be, "Help her to learn to speak gently, and firmly to her children . . . Help him to grow in perseverance . . . Help him to be more aware of the multitude of tasks his wife copes with . . . Help her to grow in her understanding of your power . . . ."

MAKE A PRAYER BOOK

When I made the decision to work at making my prayer life more fulfilling, I knew I needed a prayer book. Not because I found a scripture that said, "For a fulfilling prayer ministry thou shalt makest a book and therein write down what thou prayest for," no, I needed it because I often forgot prayer commitments. On several occasions I had sisters ask for my prayers and I would shoot off a short mini prayer at the time then promptly forget their burden. Only to be painfully reminded when I met them face to face and realized I had not been praying for them. The memory of those times was the motivation for my prayer book, but I soon discovered many other dimensions it added to my prayer ministry.

My prayer book was also the perfect place to list my thought out concerns for the people in my prayer cycle. I put each of their names at the top of a page. On that page I listed my thought out concerns and the date. Then I left room for regular status reports. Lo and behold, as I went through these concerns week after week I discovered God was granting every prayer petition but I had never seen before because I had never known how to "watch." As I looked again at the teachings on prayer I realized that we are not only told to pray we are also told to WATCH and THANK Him for the answer (Colossians 4:2).

My prayer book kept my focus on 'past' prayer requests. One of my problems had been that I would be praying fervently about one concern then a more serious or urgent one would come up. I would start focusing my prayers on it and then another one would come up that would claim my attention. In the meantime, God may have granted my request on the first, but I did not see because my attention was on the latest one. Consequently I never realized nor thanked Him for His answer. I was truly a very negligent and ungrateful child.

This book has been one of my greatest faith builders. Anytime I am tempted to become discouraged, I can glance through it and recall all the times God has rescued and blessed me and those I love. These memories quickly lift me out of any snares Satan prepares for me and fills me with confidence that my God is alive and well and taking care of me.

OVERCOMING BARRIER #2 — BE SPECIFIC

Often when we become discouraged because we don't see God answering our prayers, we begin to pray more and more in generalities. In fact, our prayer life often deteriorates into little more than the adult version of "Now I lay me down to sleep, I pray the Lord . . ." And unfortunately that only adds to our problems, because when we start resorting to generalized prayers we can't receive anything but generalized answers—that we never see.

For example, if you pray, "God please help me be a better Christian," when does the day come that you wake up ready to thank God because you are a "better" Christian? It doesn't happen. But if you pray, "Help me to discipline myself to spend time in your word daily . . . help me to pray consistently this week . . . help me to speak softly and gently to my children . . . help me to pay the electric bill . . ." then you can clearly see the result and clearly thank God for His answer. Thanking God for His answers is much more than just exercising good manners. It plays a powerful role in your overall spiritual growth. And we will discuss this aspect in more depth later.

OVERCOMING BARRIER #3 — KNOWING HOW TO PRAY

Having grown up in the Word of God, it did not occur to me that I needed to learn how to pray. After all, how much do you need to know? You just bow your head and talk to God in the name of Jesus Christ. But as I studied I realized there were many things I did not know and even more that I did not understand.

I learned there are 5 aspects of prayer mentioned in the New Testament. And for a well-balanced prayer life you need to include all five. Jesus did. He mentioned the first three (Praise, Needs, Confession) in what is known as the Lord's Prayer; He referred to the fourth (Thanksgiving) in John 11:41 and the fifth (Intercession) consumes the major portion of John 17. Let's look at the dimensions of each.

PRAISE

Praising God is a valuable tool for OUR individual spiritual growth—a rather surprising fact. Because usually praise is for the benefit of the "praisee" not the "praisor." But in God's case our knowledge of His greatness and power is so limited that we are like amateurs pointing out to a concert pianist that he does "Chopsticks" very well. And for years this awareness made me uncomfortable in my attempts at praise.

However, the example of praise is very clearly recorded in scripture, therefore, I very determinedly started to include praise in my prayer ministry. It felt unnatural at the beginning but I found reading aloud from the Psalms of praise was a comfortable alternative. Shortly, I realized the praise was not for the purpose of reminding God of His greatness; rather, it was for the purpose of reminding ME of His greatness. We all need to recall on a regular basis that: it is God's strength and protection that we must rely on, and His love, mercy and faithfulness constantly surrounds us. The consistent use of praise in our prayer life fills this need and adds dimension to our spiritual growth.

THANKSGIVING

Much of the time when our Christian walk is dull and mediocre, it is the result of not understanding or practicing the dimensions of thanksgiving (gratitude, insight and appreciation). But thanks be to God, "if we simply submit to" His commands of thanksgiving we can add these dimensions to our spiritual growth.

(1) Gratitude

The acknowledgement of Thanks not only has power and purpose in our spiritual life, it also has power and purpose in our secular life. Consider—as children we are taught to say "thank you" long before we know the meaning of the words. But the repeated use of these words not only teaches us their meaning it makes us realize that when someone serves us (whether it be with a drink of water or the opening of a door), they deserve our gratitude. Could the 12 times in the New

Testament we are told to practice thankfulness be for the same purpose—to teach us gratitude?

(2) Insight

But one of those times (1 Thessalonians 5:18, *". . . give thanks in all circumstances, for this is God's will for you in Christ Jesus . . ."*) is often difficult to implement. For there are a multitude of life experiences that are not easy to be thankful in. But it is possible when we realize that being "thankful in" and being "happy about" are not one and the same. Being "happy about" is an emotional response to our circumstance while being "thankful in" is an attitude and a behavior. The attitude is our mental approach to that event while the behavior is the literal practice of saying, "Thank you God." But how can we say, "thank you," for the loss of a loved one, the loss of a job, a flood that destroyed our uninsured furniture, carpeting, etc., etc? We often respond to such dilemmas by rationalizing, "I don't think God means be thankful for this; He just means to live my life in an overall attitude of thankfulness." And God does intend that we live our lives in an attitude of thankfulness, but no matter how many translations we read of this scripture, no matter how we twist or turn it, 1 Thessalonians 5:18 still commands, *". . . In every circumstance give thanks, for this is God's plan for you . . ."* Which means not only to live in the attitude of thankfulness but also to practice the behavior of thankfulness.

And that behavior (simply saying, "thank you for . . .") can not only draw our attention to His care in every situation but it can also teach us to see His will. A scriptural example of this concept can be found in Paul's remarks in Philippians 1:12-19. He said in effect that he now realizes his imprisonment is for the best because: 1) the guards and everyone have become aware he is imprisoned for Christ's sake, 2) other Christians are now boldly preaching Christ and 3) many Christians no longer fear being imprisoned.

Yet Paul did not want to go to prison or want to stay in prison. While there he persistently prayed to be released, and asked others to pray for his release. He prayed without doubting, for he wrote he was confident he would soon be free and be able to join them (Philippians 2:24). But he was wrong.

However, his letter to the Philippians was filled with thanksgiving, rejoicing and praise, it was also filled with insight as to how God's will was being served BY THE RESULT of Paul's imprisonment. Could it be that thanking God IN every circumstance not only focuses our attention on the blessings in each event, it also REVEALS God's use of each event in our lives.

But many of those events are painful—because God has given man the power of choice and the consequence of those choices are often tragedy. For example, the man who decides to drink, decides to drive, and accidentally kills a child. But if following such a tragedy, the parents can bow their heads and say, "Thank you for the gift of this child and the joy she was in our lives, thank you she is safely in your arms, thank you she will never feel the pain we are experiencing, thank you for all the people who comforted us during this time, thank you for the grace to forgive this man and the strength to leave his punishment or pardon in your hands, thank you for the empathy and understanding we now have of other parents who suffer such loss and the ability we will have in the future to comfort them."

In this example they are not thanking God their child is dead. They are thanking God IN the circumstance and THE RESULT is they are growing in forgiveness, strength to resist vengeance, love and empathy for others, appreciation of people's kindness, all of which are the will of God.

(3) Positive Thinking

Practicing thankfulness IN every circumstance also trains us to develop a positive attitude and become a channel for God's encouragement in the lives of others. For example, when my husband and I married, he was a new baby Christian. He was not ready to serve in many ways I wanted to. So I had the option of seizing the spiritual leadership of our family or waiting for him. I decided to wait—but what I did in fact was evaluate his spiritual shortcomings and get busy "praying them away." At the same time I sincerely (but arrogantly) chose spiritual goals for him and got busy "praying him into those." But, before he could reach one spiritual plateau, I was already praying for the next one. The result was, no matter how fast he grew, he did not measure up to my spiritual vision for him. Consequently, he was always in the shadow of failure. Eventually, God's teachings and insight convicted me of what I was doing. Consequently, I changed my thinking and my prayer life. I started thanking God for the man my husband was and all the qualities and virtues I appreciated in him. Though I said nothing to him about the change in my prayers for him, he could sense that the vibrations of criticism had changed to vibrations of appreciation. Not only did his spiritual growth go straight up but so did his confidence and achievements in many other areas.

A second example of the practical application of thanksgiving concerns one of our daughters. She married and moved to a rural area that had a small, struggling church. There were very few people her age and I was afraid she would become discouraged. I started praying fervently every day that God would not allow the situation to weaken her faith and commitment. I agonized for two years before I realized that she was not discouraged, she was not weakened in her commitment, in fact, she was thriving. I had been agonizing daily over what might happen tomorrow instead of "thanking God for what He was doing today." In both of these situations I had been focusing on the negative. Only thanking God IN each circumstance turned my negative focus into a positive one. We must never neglect thanksgiving in our prayer ministry for it is the key to a happy, confident and exciting Christian walk.

CONFESSION

Prayerful confession of our individual sins is a valuable tool for our overall spiritual growth. But Satan will try to con you out of its benefit. He whispers, "Just lump them all together, after all God knows what you've done. He even knows sins you've committed that you are unaware of." And it sounds reasonable—until you realize you are being cheated of the "overcoming power" of confession. Think about it, what is the first step an alcoholic must take to overcome his alcoholism. He must admit he is an alcoholic. He must face his problem. Confession in prayer is an even more powerful dynamic. It is to your benefit to confess to God, "Please forgive me for gossiping today, forgive me for the rumor I repeated, forgive me for the lie I told, forgive me for the resentment in my heart against my husband, etc., etc." By enumerating your sins to God, you are confronted with behaviors and attitudes in your life that need to change, problems you need to work on. And the repeated confession of some sin draws your attention to how strongly it has you bound. By way of contrast, Jesus simply says in Matthew 6:11, ". . . *forgive us of our sins as we forgive those that sin against us . . .*" but remember Jesus had NO individual sins so the real focus of His statement was forgiveness—God's forgiveness of us and our forgiveness of others. The most specific scripture in the New Testament concerning confession of sin in prayer is found in 1 John 1:9, ". . . *If we confess our sins, he is faithful and just to forgive us our sins, and to cleanse us from all unrighteousness . . .*" It is comforting to know that confession not only opens the door to overcoming, but even more importantly—it opens the door to forgiveness.

SUPPLICATION

For most people the number one cause of anxiety is concern over their needs being met. But as Christians we can live above that level of anxiety. Paul said in Philippians 4:6, ". . . *Have no anxiety about anything, but in everything by prayer and supplication with thanks-*

giving let your requests be made known to God . . ." And the next verse says, *". . . And the peace of God, which passes all understanding, will keep your hearts and your minds in Christ Jesus . . ."* The key to peace of mind (or freedom from anxiety) is to ask God for whatever you need, then (1) ACCEPT WHAT COMES AS HIS ANSWER AND (2) BE CONTENT WITH IT. God's response to our requests is similar to ours when our children ask for something, ice cream for instance. We give it to them, IF they have not already had too many sweets, IF it will not make them sick, IF they have eaten the foods their bodies need for proper nutrition, etc., etc. When we ask God to meet our needs (food, clothing, shelter, etc) He responds as any trustworthy parent and gives us what is best for us at that time. How do I know? Because in Matthew 7:9-11 Jesus says, *". . . Or what man of you, if his son asks him for bread, will give him a stone? Or if he asks for a fish, will give him a serpent? If you then, who are evil, know how to give good gifts to your children, how much more will your Father who is in heaven give good things to those who ask him! . . ."* But just like children we often are not satisfied with what God provides. We want it bigger and better like the child who cries for a 3-dip cone (he can't handle) instead of the 1-dip cone (he can handle). Paul said in Philippians 4:11, *". . . Not that I complain of want; for I have learned, in whatever state I am, to be content . . ."* Paul says contentment is something he learned. And that is encouraging because if he learned it so can we, if we take the same mental approach. And his mental approach was, 'I can live in whatever state God provides for me because Jesus Christ is going to empower me to do so.'

INTERCESSION

The prayer of intercession is the most frequently mentioned prayer in the New Testament. I do not believe this was accidental—because of all aspects of prayer it is the one that focuses on the needs of others. And that is the focus of the New Testament—others. Praise in prayer focuses your attentions on the greatness and adequacy of God —Confession, Thanksgiving and Supplication focuses your attention on you—while Intercession forces your attention on the needs of others. It is easy to become self-absorbed in prayer. Constantly engrossed in: "What I need to change in my life . . . How weak I am . . . How short I fall . . . What I need here . . . What I need there . . . Being thankful for helping ME with this . . . For helping ME with that . . ."

But intercessory prayer turns our attention to the needs of others. It makes us aware that: (1) I am not the only person that has difficulties and, (2) I am not the only person with needs that have not been met. The dynamic power of intercessory prayer is three faceted. When

48

my heart is right in intercessory prayer, two facets benefit me and one facet benefits the person I am praying for. The first facet that benefits me is the obvious one mentioned above—focusing on the needs of others. This protects me from self-absorption and challenges me to grow spiritually through actively trying to lift the burdens of others. The second facet that benefits me goes into operation when I obey the command to, ". . . pray for your enemies. . . ." This exciting aspect of prayer benefits me in several ways: 1) It gives me insight. If my heart is right in this prayer, it should convict me of any guilt I have in the conflict. For it is difficult to be petty, overly sensitive, or vindictive while kneeling at God's feet in prayer. 2) It helps me overcome my own evil. The 12th chapter of Romans discusses conflict with others and one of the points it makes is in verse 21, ". . . do not be overcome by evil, but instead overcome evil with good . . ." Through praying for someone that has actually wronged you, you can overcome the strong human desire for revenge. And through obeying Proverbs 25:21,22 concerning behavior toward an enemy, ". . . if your enemy is hungry, feed him; if he is thirsty, give him a drink . . ." (returning kind behavior for unkind behavior) you can overcome any feelings of anger and resentment.

It focuses my attention on the "problems" my enemy has and helps me develop a merciful attitude toward him. (Consider Jesus example on the cross.) When we pray for an enemy it does not mean they will not receive recompense for their sin. Their pardon is between them and God, but praying for them helps us to forgive them and overcome any bitterness or evil that would otherwise make us useless in God's service. There is a dynamic power in intercessory prayer that is far beyond my understanding. Obviously, an affirmative answer to prayer does not depend on the number of people praying. But the word of God is filled with examples of Christians praying for one another and requesting the prayers of one another. Paul, a man who had been blessed with many spiritual gifts and was being used by God in a mighty way still wrote to simple, everyday Christians and asked them to pray for him (Romans 15:30-32; 2 Corinthians 1:11; Ephesians 6:19,20; 2 Thessalonians 3:1). Why? The implication is clear: the power of prayer is magnified as more Christians request the same thing. So, praying for others and requesting the prayers of others is not just a "nice" or "sweet" thing to do—it is a powerful thing to do. A powerful thing that can actually change life for someone else and at the same time change life for you. But you can do all of this and still have a dismal prayer ministry UNLESS you have learned to recognize God's answers to your prayers and the next chapter deals with that dimension for spiritual growth in prayer.

DISCUSSION QUESTIONS

1. What point in this section had the most impact on you? Why?
2. What interferes with your time in prayer?
3. How can you overcome it?
4. Discuss Luke 18:1; Philippians 4:6; James 1:5-7; James 5:16.

When the Problem
With Prayer Is Me

Part 2
WATCH FOR GOD'S ANSWERS

In Prayer - Part 1, we discussed how to overcome the first three barriers to a Powerful Prayer Ministry. In this chapter, we will look at the fourth and most difficult obstacle: LEARNING TO SEE GOD'S ANSWERS TO PRAYER. We can practice and benefit from everything we learned in Prayer - Part 1 but if we have not learned to recognize God's answers to our prayer petitions, we will (on many occasions) experience a mediocre and discouraging Christian walk. And, consequently, a mediocre and discouraging spiritual growth.

KNOW THE SCRIPTURES ON PRAYER

The foundation for 'recognizing' God's answers to prayer is to know the scriptures on prayer. There are 27 examples of God answering prayer in the New Testament. There are 5 passages that enumerate behaviors that will hinder prayer (1 Peter 3:7; 1 John 3:22; Mark 11:25; James 1:7,8; 4:3). But all the examples and passages in the New Testament could be summed up by 1 John 3:22, ". . . And whatsoever we ask, we receive of him, because we keep his commandments, and do those things that are pleasing in His sight . . ."

This does not mean we must be sinless to receive from God, but it does mean we must be serious about our commitment. Assuming we understand these passages and what a "serious commitment to God" is, let's look at how God answers prayer.

WATCH FOR ORDINARY ANSWERS

God answers prayer—He answers it "yes" or He answers it "no." The "no" answers aren't difficult to recognize. It is the "yes" answers that often confuse us. Often because we limit God to "out-of-the-ordinary" answers, like parting the sea and walking on water. But from looking at Matthew 7:7; 1 John 3:22; Philippians 4:6, we can conclude that for God to grant our prayer petitions is ordinary—not extraordinary—so watch for "ordinary answers." How? Learn to recognize His providential care.

ANSWERS OFTEN COME
THROUGH PROVIDENTIAL CARE

We are often like the young woman who saw a work for the Lord on the other side of a stream. She did not know how to swim so she bowed her head and prayed for a bridge. When she raised her head a few minutes later, there was no bridge. But the water level had lowered and some stones appeared crossing the stream—but she didn't see them because she was looking for a bridge. She bowed her head and prayed again . . . she raised her head — no bridge. But in the meantime lightning had struck a tree and it had fallen across the stream. But she didn't see it, she was looking for a bridge. She bowed her head and prayed again . . . some beavers completed a dam that crossed the stream but when she raised her head she didn't see it because it wasn't a "bridge."

She sat down feeling frustrated and discouraged. She didn't understand—she knew it would be God's will for her to do this work. Yet He wasn't providing a bridge. It just seemed that her plans to serve God never worked out.

Then she heard the rattle, rattle, bang, bang of a truck and construction crew driving up. The men jumped out of the truck with picks and shovels and started building a bridge, right at her feet. She smiled in relief and then happily prayed, "Dear heavenly father, you don't need to worry any more about the bridge, the Highway Department is going to build it."

Does God really provide in such ordinary/providential ways? The 11th chapter of Numbers says He does. It tells how God through ordinary/providential means answered a request (actually a complaint).

This chapter tells how the children of Israel were complaining in the wilderness because they were tired of eating manna—they wanted meat. Verse 31 tells us God caused a wind to blow that brought quail from the seashore and dropped them in the camp until they were several feet deep. God did not zap quail that had previously been nonexistent into the camp. Instead He brought them from their natural habitat by the sea on a strong wind (another natural part of life) to answer this request.

BUT WE MUST HAVE EYES OF FAITH

But we must have eyes of faith to see His answers. Someone who disbelieves or whose faith is weak would look at this same story and explain it this way: "What happened is no great mystery. There was simply an abundance of quail in the area by the sea that year. And when a high pressure system up near Macedonia came rushing south and collided with a strong low pressure system moving up from Egypt, naturally, winds of hurricane force developed. They literally picked up the quail, who had no protection on the shores, and blew them several hundred miles into the wilderness. When the winds subsided the birds were exhausted. They fell to the earth, right in the middle of a nomad camp. You should have seen those nomads—they thought their God did it. But in our enlightened age we know better—it was just a combination of abnormal conditions.

But God says HE DID IT. We often have the desire of faith and can ask without doubting. But we don't have the eyes of faith because when it comes to receiving, we doubt God was responsible. We tend to credit a "combination of circumstances."

DOORBELLS, PHONE CALLS AND PLAIN BROWN ENVELOPES

We must always be watchful for God's answers because they often arrive through a simple, routine phone call, doorbell or plain brown envelope.

For example, have you ever prayed, "Lead me to some soul today, Oh teach me Lord just what to say" And then become irritated when: (1) your neighbor, whose life is a constant mess, comes over and spends the morning talking to you. You get so frustrated because the day is slipping away. And you had planned to call the church secretary and get the name of someone to visit, or, (2) your mother-in-law (who is not a Christian) calls and wants you to go shopping. You know she is going to gripe about this, complain about that, and go on and on about her loneliness since her husband died. You just don't feel up to it. Besides, you wanted to practice "pure, undefiled religion" today by visiting some widows and orphans. In fact, you've even talked to your class teacher about ministering in this area. But you can't seem to get started because of all these interruptions.

Someone (I don't know who) christened these obstructions as "Divine Interruptions." As we grow in spiritual maturity, we recognize them as such and thank God. And we learn to adjust OUR plans to serve Him—to accommodate HIS plans for our service.

Jesus recognized this type of opportunity. Remember the woman at the well in John 4. Meeting her interfered with His plan to go to Jerusalem. He could have irritably noted that she wasn't even a good candidate to share God's message with. Her life was a mess, her initial response to Him was one of ridicule, and she tried to change the subject when He attempted to talk about her needs. And if taking time with her wasn't enough, He ended up stuck there for three more days teaching the rest of her village.

But this story is not told with irritation in the New Testament. It is told with victory and joy because it is treated as a "Divine Delay" instead of one more interruption in Jesus' plans.

Ordinary answers to prayer not only come in the ring of a telephone or doorbell—they often come in plain, brown envelopes. For example, our phone billing got put into the wrong computer billing cycle one time and we kept getting cut off notices almost before we got the bill. Yet, it was not showing on their computer that way. Consequently, we were asked to put up a large deposit. And though we were very indignant, our choices were to remove the phone, pay the deposit or sue. The most practical choice was to pay the deposit. Shortly after, the phone company discovered the billing cycle error and corrected it—but our deposit was already in the computer and could not be returned for six months.

Six months later, due to the most unlikely set of circumstances, we had some enormous bills hit all at once. Remarkably though, at the same time, we had sums of money arriving in plain, brown envelopes from the most unexpected sources: the return of the phone bill deposit, refunds on electric pumping bills paid 15 years before, funds from the sale of cotton placed in a co-op 17 years before, refunds on ginning fees from 16 years before, an unexpected raise, etc., etc.

We were humbled to realize that God had been preparing for this need long before we knew we had it. Just as the abundance of quail by the seashore was prepared before the Israelites complained about the manna. Thank God for His care.

WE MUST NOT BE BLINDED BY FEAR

But sometimes fear and worry blind us to God's power. There is an example of this type of blindness in 2 Kings 6:8-22. It tells of the king of Aram who sent an army down to Dothan to capture Elisha. They surrounded the city one night. The next morning when Elisha's servant awoke and went out on the balcony, he saw the enemy army and was terrified.

But when Elisha came onto the balcony and saw the surrounding army, he was not afraid because he had eyes of faith. He prayed for God to open his servant's eyes. The Lord did. Then the servant saw on the surrounding mountains (behind the enemy army) the Lord's army with horses and chariots of fire. Needless to say, the Lord fought Elisha's battle for him. And the story has a happy ending for, even the enemy army—read it. But the servant might have died of fright if God had not opened his eyes.

We are often like Elisha's servant. We see a problem looming so large that our fear of it completely blinds us to God's ability to deliver us—in any situation.

A practical example I recall concerns a young mother whose husband had deserted her and her two children. She had no job skills, no money and no family to help her. We got her into a job training program and money to meet her basic necessities. But just when we thought everything was arranged, she received a disconnect notice from the utility company. They were going to disconnect her electricity because (unknown to her) her husband had left a $700 electric bill. This was the final blow. She was seized first with fear and then with despair. It seemed hopeless; there was no escape.

But, lo and behold, her husband's uncle (whom she barely knew) heard of her plight. He came and paid the electric bill and made arrangements to give her future help until she could get on her feet. This had to be God's army—come in answer to our very fervent prayers.

PRAYER ALWAYS CHANGES THINGS

The first rule we must master to see God's answer to prayer is: PRAYER ALWAYS CHANGES THINGS. We are assured of this in Matthew 7:7 when Jesus said: ask, it will be given; seek—ye shall find; knock—it will be opened unto you. Then He explains why. He says that if man, being evil, knows how to give good gifts to his children when they ask, how much more will God give us good things when we ask. This passage is teaching: we can rely on God responding to our requests.

And the most important clue to seeing those responses is to know that prayer always changes things. But we can easily miss them unless we realize that many of those changes may not be what WE had in mind. (Remember the young woman at the stream.)

A dramatic example of such an answer could have easily been overlooked if my friend and I had not learned the value of comparing the changes in our lives to the petitions we were taking to God. Her life had been difficult. It had been a downhill roller coaster ride through two marriages and two divorces, discouragement, depression, despair, analysis and suicide attempts. And her children had been with her all the way.

Then she came for counseling and met Jesus Christ. She became a Christian and life took on a whole new meaning for her. But she had taught her teenagers 'established' religion was shallow, empty and had nothing to offer. Now when she tried to teach them differently, they

55

were suspicious and skeptical.

She agonized in prayer over them. The agony was even greater because she knew she was responsible for their attitude. One day she called, especially down because her younger son (whom life had been the hardest for) had been dropped from the basketball team. Her heart was breaking for him because she felt the basketball team was the one joy he had in life, now even it was gone.

I felt for both of them, but had no answer when she asked how God could let this happen when he had already been through so much. I asked her to review her "thought out" prayers for him. The most urgent of these was her request for him to know Jesus. In an effort to bring this about she had been taking him to church with her. We both suspected he rather enjoyed it—but did not want to admit it because his friends on the team did not attend church.

About a week later she called, absolutely elated. She had come in from work to find him and two new friends working on Algebra II. At the same time they were talking to a girl on the phone and having a great time. Later, she discovered the new friends all went to church and were excited about their faith.

The point for this lesson is: she was praying for him to know Jesus, but the best circumstances for that happening resulted in the temporary pain of not making the team. This was not the method she anticipated God using to answer her prayer. And if she had not checked this "change" against her petitions, she would have probably "gone away sorrowful" convinced that life had dealt this son one more low blow.

GOD SOMETIMES HAS A DILEMMA
GRANTING OUR PETITIONS

We are sometimes like a teenager who asks her mother to help her lose 10 pounds. In order to do that, the mother must withhold certain foods or get her daughter to exercise more. But the daughter really doesn't want to do either. She doesn't want to walk two miles to school because she will be all sweaty. She doesn't want to take P.E. because her hair will look 'gross' afterwards. And she doesn't like any foods other than hamburgers, french fries, chips and dip, cokes and ice cream. The mother has a dilemma. If she gives her daughter the cookies and ice cream she pleads for after school and the hamburgers and fries she wants for supper, then she can't grant the long range request—the weight loss. We often do the same thing to God.

We ask to be more patient—but we don't want to deal with any trials that produce patience. We ask to be more loving—but we don't

want to make any sacrifices that help us develop a more loving attitude. We want to be stronger—but we don't want to carry any burdens. We want to know the Bible—but we don't want to spend the
time to study. We want to lead others to Christ—but we are too embarrassed to talk about Jesus, etc., etc.

DOES PRAYER CHANGE THINGS
WHEN GOD SAYS "NO"?

There are two examples in the Bible where God said "no" to people
He loved. God heard their prayers and things changed but not in the
way they desired. Look at Paul in 2 Corinthians 12:7-10. Paul asked
God to remove his thorn in the flesh. He asked three times. What
happened? He was left with the thorn. But his prayer changed things:
(1) God gave him grace and strength to deal with it, (2) Paul learned to
appreciate weakness, because he learned God is made perfect in weakness, and (3) he realized the thorn was serving a purpose in his overall
spiritual growth.

Anytime God says "no" to you in a prayer request you can be certain that: (1) He will give you the grace and strength to cope with your
problem, (2) that God's image will be perfected in your struggle, and
(3) the thorn is serving an overall purpose in your life or the life of
someone else.

A second example of God saying "no" is to Christ in the garden.
Jesus begged God to let the cup of crucifixion pass from him. And
God had the power to do it; He could have brought about man's
redemption in some other way. Or He could have zapped Christ with a
body that would not feel the pain of the ordeal . . . but he didn't.
Because Christ put God in a dilemma. He was praying, ". . . let this
cup pass . . . if it be Your will . . ." God's will was that man's
redemption come about through the death of Jesus and that He bear
the pain. So by answering that part of Christ's prayer, God could not
grant the first (even though Jesus knew He would if He but asked).

But God did answer the prayer with more than a "no" answer.
As Christ agonized in the garden—God sent angels to minister to His
needs. And when the soldiers came (God's answer to Christ's plea),
Christ did not have to be drug away. He went to the trial and the cross
with dignity. For God's grace was sufficient and He was given the
strength to bear what He must bear.

DISCUSSION QUESTIONS

1. What point in this section had the most impact on you?

2. Discuss Jonah 2:1-7. How did Jonah get in this situation? How did he get out?

3. Are we ardent in prayer during times of trouble and negligent when things are going 'okay'?

4. Discuss Luke 23:42. What attitude did the thief display in his petition?

5. If Jesus and the Father were one, why do you think Jesus spent so much time in prayer?

Chapter Five

Discover Your Talents and Your Ministry

One of the requirements for reaching our full spiritual potential is discovering and multiplying our talents. But few of us are totally confident we are doing that. In fact, we often live for years uncertain about our service to God, plagued with such thoughts as:

(1) "Am I really serving God in the way He wants? Should I be serving as a missionary, or working as a houseparent in some children's home, or doing the work of a foster parent, etc., etc., etc?" Or, we wonder,

(2) "Am I burying a talent God has given me? Is it possible I could teach like . . . or bring people to Christ like . . . or have a music ministry . . . if I just put in more effort?" Or, we lament,

(3) "I wish I knew what my talent is. I want to serve more effectively, but I can't because I haven't found my talent." Or, perhaps we think,

(4) "I don't have any special talent. There isn't a thing I can do that a hundred others can't do if they just try."

Such thinking indicates that we are falling short of our spiritual potential and into one of Satan's best traps. For such thinking can become totally SELF-absorbing. We can get so hung-up searching for some elusive talent and worrying about what God wants us to do that we are useless in His service. But how can we avoid it? After all, we do need to use our talents for God don't we? Yes, because as we use them in His service, not only do they bring glory to God, they activate a threefold blessing in our lives. They: grow and multiply making our lives more fruitful and rewarding, direct our steps in the ministry God has designed for each of us, and lead us toward our full spiritual potential.

But we don't have to get all hung-up "finding" our talents, for God has provided a way to spotlight them for us. Consider the parable Jesus told in Matthew 25:14-30. In this passage Jesus begins by saying a man was going on a journey. He called his servants and entrusted his property to them. (He does not say he called "some" of them, it says he called his servants, implying all.) The man gave one of the servants 5 talents of money, one 2 talents of money and the last 1 talent, each according to his ability. (Notice: he GAVE the talents. He did not hide them somewhere on the property or on their person for them to find. Their talents seemed to be out in the open for them and everyone else to see.)

The first two servants went immediately (no procrastinating) and put their money to work and doubled it. The third servant buried his in the ground where it would be safe. Later, the master returned for an accounting. The first two servants had doubled their money, and even though the 5-talent servant had gained more than the 2-talent servant they were both praised and rewarded equally. For they had done the best they could with what they had. Next, the master called the 1-talent servant. He began by explaining, "I knew you were a hard man, harvesting where you have not sown and gathering where you have not scattered seed. So I was afraid . . . and hid your money." Then he returned the one talent safe and undamaged. But the master was not pleased. He admitted he expected results and pointed out that since the servant knew this, he should have made even greater effort to multiply his money.

So the Lord commanded the talent be taken from the fearful servant and gave it to the ten-talent servant. Then the master made a statement that seemed unfair, "For everyone who has will be given more, and he will have an abundance. Whoever does not have, even what he had will be taken from him." But actually, this statement is not unfair—it is just practical. The world recognizes this same concept and states it this way: "If you want a job done, give it to a busy man." In this parable the talent given to each servant was money (or something of value). But we can quickly see that we could substitute "a special ability" for a "talent of money" and this parable would be just as true in every way.

BUT HOW DOES THIS HELP US KNOW WHAT OUR TALENTS ARE?

One more application of this parable will spotlight our individual talents and our ministry. All we need to do is replace the phrase "talent of money" with the word "opportunity." In which case a paraphrase of the parable would go something like this, "When the master prepared to go on a long journey he called his servants to him and gave them various opportunities, EACH ACCORDING TO HIS ABILITIES. (See they already had the talent to meet the opportunities. Matthew 25:15.) To one he gave five opportunities. To another he gave two opportunities. And to the last one he gave one opportunity . . . We can easily see how the parable would develop: as each servant used an opportunity he would receive more opportunities and consequently develop more abilities. When he refused an opportunity, he would be closing the door to a whole area of service. Therefore, our God-given opportunities are like spotlights focusing on potential or talents that others see in us. And as we accept these opportunities, they will double and double and double again. First thing we know we have a ministry.

IS THERE SCRIPTURAL SUPPORT FOR THIS THEORY?

Yes, there is scriptural support for this theory. In Ephesians 2:10 we are told, "For we are God's workmanship in Christ Jesus, created to do good works, which God prepared in advance for us to do." And John 12:7 is a good example of such a ". . . work prepared in advance . . ." In that passage, Mary anointed Jesus' feet with an expensive perfume. When she was criticized, Jesus said, ". . . It was meant that she should save this perfume for the day of my burial . . ." The phrase, "it was meant" clearly shows this was a work prepared in advance and Mary was given the opportunity and the capability (she owned the perfume) to accomplish it.

The gospels speak often of Martha and Mary. And we can easily see the talents they possessed in John 11 and 12. Martha appears to have had organizational and leadership qualities which she used particularly in hospitality. While Mary seemed to be more sensitive to Jesus' teachings and His needs. But the "spotlight" that draws these talents to our attention is the opportunities they received to use them.

Consider Stephen, whom we meet first in Acts. We are told he was full of the Spirit, but hundreds of others were too. However, the apostles must have seen organizational and administrative skills in him along with the heart and spirit of a godly man. So he was given this opportunity to serve, which he accepted. Later we see he developed into an evangelist boldly preaching the gospel. Could this have been the multiplication of a talent?

The Apostles themselves are all excellent examples of opportunity "spotlighting" potential and talent. From everything we read, there was nothing in these men's background to qualify them for the work

61

of an Apostle (except Paul). But Jesus saw the potential and after hours of prayer, He selected them from among His followers. There were probably other disciples with more social and political prestige. But Jesus saw in these 12 men, the talents and qualities needed to fulfill the work of an Apostle.

If we go back to Matthew 25:14 again and read the parable remembering that the opportunities were given ACCORDING TO EACH MAN'S ABILITIES, we can see that God does not give an opportunity that you do not already have the talent to perform. So when you are approached, provided or confronted with an opportunity, take it—if you do not already have the ability, you have the potential to develop it. In fact, the scriptures do not say, "Go find your talent (special ability) and come put it to work for the Lord." Instead, we are told time and again to take every God-given opportunity (Galatians 6:10; Colossians 4:5; Ephesians 5:16).

Now, note that the parable beginning in Matthew 25:31, just below the parable of the talents, leaves no doubts whatsoever about the use of opportunity. Remember, the parable is describing the day of judgment. And the Son is dividing the saved from the lost. He says, to the saved, "... for I was ... and you did ..." To the lost He says, "... for I was ... and you did not ..." He did not say, "Enter in because you built the biggest church in New York City ... were the best teacher in Texas ... were the best speaker in the brotherhood ..." No, he said the saved responded to their opportunities ("you saw") to meet peoples' needs—the lost did not. If this is a criteria for judgment we can be sure we are all receiving opportunities to serve, but we often miss them for a multitude of reasons.

WE ARE OFTEN BLIND
TO OUR OPPORTUNITIES

(1) We are often blind to our own opportunities or abilities because we are busy looking at someone else's. We see them do this or that. We hear them praised and admired. We long to have their abilities and opportunities. And as we watch through various shades of envy, our own opportunities slip by unnoticed. We have such an example in Acts 8. Simon the Sorcerer was converted to Jesus. He was already a man of great influence and evidently gifted with qualities of leadership, for we are told many people followed him. But he saw that "... *through the laying on of the Apostles hands the Holy Ghost was given* ..." and he wanted that ability. He even offered to buy it. After he was told to repent, we hear no more about him. It is sad that he did not see his own opportunity. He was already a gifted man of influence

and leadership. What a man of God he could have been, if he had not been overtaken with envy and greed as he looked at the gifts and opportunities of others.

(2) Sometimes, we may see and even recognize an opportunity but fail to grasp it for it differs from what we had in mind. We have an example of this reaction in Matthew 19:16-22. Jesus gave a young man an opportunity. He told him to sell what he had and come follow him. And the scripture says he went away sorrowful, ". . . for he had much goods . . ." This young man was a dedicated servant. He had kept the commandments from his youth up and he even went to Jesus to find out how to be more diligent in his service. But when Jesus told him how, he turned away and we hear no more about him in scripture. I wonder what kind of ministry he missed.

(3) Another reason we often miss our opportunities is because we are too impatient. We want to do this mighty work for Jesus or that mighty work for Jesus—right now. We don't want to wait or prepare or let God take the lead. Jesus, Himself, almost fell into this trap in Luke 2:40-52 when he stayed behind at the Temple talking with the teachers. Evidently, He was doing a remarkable job, because the teachers were impressed. The promise and potential was already evident in His life. But Jesus was running ahead of God's plan for Him, because His parents, (whom God had selected and entrusted His care to) came and took Him home with them. It was not until eighteen years later that His ministry actually began. And then it was His mother who insisted He perform His first miracle. (Could that have been God's direction just as taking Him home at age 12 must have been?)

(4) On many other occasions we miss opportunities and even exciting ministries because we just don't recognize them. Our negative attitudes disguise them and we see only problems—never realizing they are God-given opportunities. In fact, any problem we see is just the back-side of an opportunity. For example: 1) We may see the church we attend is negligent about greeting and talking to visitors. The members rejoice so much in one another's company that they visit together and never get around to greeting and talking with visitors. If you've seen this problem in your congregation, then you have the talent to do something about it. Not only do you have the talent, God is also giving you the opportunity. You can become the friendliest, quickest-to-talk-to-a-visitor member of your congregation.

SATAN WILL TRY TO STOP YOU

But such opportunities often come to naught because they are so effective, Satan has surrounded them with snares. And one of his most deceiving is the NO-ONE-WILL-HELP-ME-SNARE. For instance, we decide to be friendly, so we rush to the back on Sunday morning after dismissal. We catch two or three visitors and speak to them, a little awkwardly, but we have made an effort. We see others heading toward their cars. We are sure no one has spoken to them. So, we mount a soap box and start a campaign to get everyone to do what we are. What happens—nothing! Our brethren just keep talking among themselves and ignore the visitors. Before long, we get frustrated, discouraged and decide that if no one is going to help us—forget it. See how Satan has trapped us? He has taken our mind off the opportunity: our chance to encourage visitors to return to our service and seek Jesus. Instead we are focusing on how our brethren are letting us, God, and the world down; never realizing that we have started letting all of them down. Instead of our example influencing all of them, their example has influenced us.

Another one of Satan's most successful snares is the BUT-I-DON'T-HAVE-THE-AUTHORITY trap. We are hesitant to do anything that we have not been given someone's verbal permission or authority to do. But we don't need permission or authority to do the Lord's work. We just need that to start programs. For example, God tells us to encourage, so we have His authority and permission to be the friendliest, most encouraging person in the lobby after every service. But we don't have the authority to stand up and tell the congregation that everyone whose name starts with the letter A-G must go to the lobby the first Sunday of the month and greet visitors. Then on the second Sunday, the H-M's are the official greeters, etc. That is a program. And programs need the leadership's permission and authority.

Another problem we might see: the elderly in our congregation tend to be forgotten. This problem has a beautiful opportunity on the other side. We can invite the elderly over to our homes for ice cream and cookies, or for an outing of some sort. We can have a fellowship for them, etc., etc.—We could go on and on endlessly listing problems that we "might" see in our congregations. But God does not hold us responsible for "might-be" problems. We are just responsible for the ones we actually see and the way we react to them. For they are the opportunities and ministries God is "spotlighting" for us.

Right about here it is easy to object with, "Oh, sure, I see problems, in fact, I see so very many problems that I can't possibly work on all of them. I don't have that much time." After I realized that every problem was an opportunity and started working on it, I soon discovered the busier I was, the fewer problems I saw. Yes, my ministry multiplied—but it multiplied in a definite direction. As a result, I did not see as many "other" problems. That is when I found that work is the best antidote for complaints. But Satan does his best to hide this knowledge from us with all sorts of rationales. Because he does not want us to become aware that God is spotlighting an exciting ministry that can lead us on to our spiritual potential.

I AM A LIVING EXAMPLE

I am a living example of someone resisting a ministry God was planning. To put it honestly, God had to drag me toward my ministry for years. Because I had planned a different ministry, I wanted to be a missionary or a social worker, or a children's home houseparent, or take in foster children, or write Agatha Christie-type mysteries, etc., etc. And I really put effort into pursuing those areas of service. And God attempted to gently close those doors—but knowing me He eventually had to slam them, and drag me toward the doors (opportunities) He had been holding open for me. Doors that I didn't see because I was so busy deciding how God and I were going to get His program on the road.

Now, I praise God for the love that moved Him to stay with me. Patiently, picking me up after each and every disappointment when I was trying so hard and accomplishing so little. And for the love that heard me finally say in frustration, "Okay, I don't understand. I have tried to do this . . . and it didn't work. I tried to do that . . . and it didn't work. I tried to do something else . . . and it didn't work either. Now you show me! I am going to let you bring me opportunities. And I am going to take every one that comes along. So please, don't bring me one you don't want me to take." And praise God, He heard my prayer and my ministry took off. God took all the knowledge I had been accumulating and used it—but in a different area than I had planned. He took every skill I had been developing (typing, writing, research, teaching) and gave me glorious opportunities to use them. He took every experience (good and bad) and gave me fresh insight into His plans for me.

And He took my life and my ministry and multiplied them a thousand times over. He built them into more than I even had the courage to pray for.

IN CONCLUSION

He is a glorious God. And if He can lead me to an exciting ministry through the opportunities He provides, He can lead you. But get ready! Your life may take off in the most unbelievable directions.

Or, he may keep you simmering for a while longer because you are not ready for what He has in mind. But you can be sure of this—He has you in His mind. For Paul said in Ephesians 2:10, ". . . *For we are God's workmanship, created in Christ Jesus to do good works; which God prepared in advance for us to do.*"

DISCUSSION QUESTIONS

1. What point in this lesson had the most impact on you? Why?
2. What opportunities have you had in God's service in the last year? What talents or potential did they spotlight?
3. What were talent or special abilities given for in the church? (Ephesians 4:11-16)
4. Discuss Romans 12:6-10. How is serving, showing mercy, encouraging, etc. a talent or special ability?

Chapter Six
You Are
Your Brother's Keeper

Reaching your spiritual potential means becoming more like Jesus Christ. And there is no area of spiritual growth that more dramatically imitates Him than the area of "loving one another." Jesus intended for us to follow His example in this facet of spiritual growth when He said in John 13:34, *"...A new commandment I give you: Love one another. As I have loved you, so you must love one another..."* This verse clearly teaches that Jesus wants us to respond to one another as He responded to His disciples.

As we look at Jesus and His disciples in their interaction, one aspect that clearly stands out is the spiritual responsibility Jesus displayed for His disciples. Yet we rarely see it exhibited among brethren today. The more prevalent attitude is: "Who am I to take spiritual responsibility for someone else? I'm just barely making it myself. Anyway, who made me their keeper...?" Jesus did when He said, *"...Love one another as I have loved you..."* With this command He made us, to a degree, one another's keeper. And the degree of responsibility involved becomes clear when we look at the ways Jesus loved His disciples.

WHEN THE COMMAND WAS GIVEN

Let's look at the circumstances that existed when Jesus first gave this command (John 13:34). (1) He was preparing His disciples for His departure so He said, *"...My children, I will be with you only a little longer. You will look for me, and just as I told the Jews, so I tell you now: Where I am going, you cannot come..."* (John 13:33), then He told them to love one another. We can identify with His message here. Remember times we have had to be away from our families? Invariably, we leave them with the words, "Be sure to love and help one another while I am away." And the fact His parting words were so similar make us realize how close His ties were to His disciples.

(2) He had not yet died for them. When we consider this scripture, "...love one another as I have loved you..." we often relate it to being willing to die for one another. But at the time Jesus gave this command He had not died. Yet the scripture says, "...As I have loved..." Notice that phrase is past tense. If He had not died, then what had He done to show His love?

HOW HAD CHRIST LOVED THEM?

In the gospels we see Jesus displaying His love for man time and time again. But as we analyze His love we can see it exhibited in five different ways:

a)He reached out to initiate the love. In other words, He took the first step. He did not wait for humanity to get together, take a vote and decide they needed a redeemer. Instead, God saw a need and responded. And Jesus continued this pattern on earth. For example, Matthew 15:32, the people had followed Him for 3 days and He realized they needed food before He sent them away. So he took what they had to offer and blessed and multiplied it to meet their needs. The gospels are full of such examples. Nearly all believers will help others WHEN THEY ARE ASKED. But Jesus offers His help before He is asked. He initiated His love then to mankind, to His disciples and He is still initiating it today to you and me.

b) As we follow Jesus we see Him loving men compassionately. When He saw others in pain He grieved with them. The most dramatic example of His empathy can be found in John 11:33,34. It is found in the story of His friend Lazarus. There Jesus had been called to His friend's bedside—but He did not come until four days after Lazarus' death. The dead man's sisters and friends were in mourning when Jesus arrived. Verse 33 describes the scene, "...When Jesus saw her weeping, and the Jews who had come along with her also weeping, he was deeply moved in spirit and troubled..." then verse 35 states, "...Jesus wept..."

On this occasion He knew their grief would soon be over, He knew Lazarus would be raised from the dead in minutes—but He hurt because they hurt. What a comforting thought. We all recall shedding tears that turned out to be for nought. But we can be sure that even then Jesus hurt with us. Because His love is a love of compassion.

c) We also see Jesus loving with a "serving" love. Service is a part of love just as love is a part of service. The two cannot be separated.

Consider, one of the strongest loves we will ever experience is the love we have for our children and mates. Yet, there is no one that we will ever have to serve more. It was probably by design that Jesus gave this command just after He had washed His disciples' feet. Chapter 13 starts with, *"...It was just before the Passover Feast. Jesus knew that the time had come for him to leave this world and go to the Father. Having loved his own who were in the world, he now showed them the full extent of his love..."* The next 16 verses describe one of the ways He showed them the *"...full extent of his love..."* He served them not in a martyr's death but in the lowly task of washing their feet. This is even more amazing when we remember that He was aware that He had only a few hours to live. Under these circumstances, He would have been perfectly justified to let them serve Him. But instead, He *"...showed them the full extent of his love..."* by taking this time to serve them.

d) He also had an instructive love. Jesus never ignored or neglected an opportunity to teach. He was always sensitive to teaching opportunities whether in a crowd or one-to-one. A typical example is in John 4—with the woman at the well. He was tired, dirty, hungry, and thirsty. He could have easily excused Himself on those conditions alone—but He did not. In addition, she was a Samaritan and would not be open to a Jew teaching her. Plus, this woman had lived a rather scarlet life and would hardly be interested in religion. Three reasonable excuses for letting this teaching opportunity go by—but He did not. No matter what the circumstances, He always reached out to share salvation.

e) Jesus loved people "honestly." Often, this is the most difficult aspect of His love to imitate. Because it is easy to behave rudely and unkindly while self-righteously thinking we are being "honest." (An example was my grandmother. She felt that if she did not like your hair a certain way, or thought you looked a little plumper, or thought your dress was tacky, she was duty bound to tell you—because she was honest.) But that is not the "honest" love that Jesus portrayed. He loved honestly by loving the person in the way they needed—which was not always the way they wanted. For example, the woman at the well wanted to discuss 'religion.' Jesus insisted on dealing with her problem, *"...Go, call your husband and come back...I have no husband...You are right when you say you have no husband. The fact is, you have had five husbands, and the man you now have is not your husband. What you have just said is quite true..."* He went straight to the problem. And He must have stayed there until it was resolved because we know she accepted Christ as the Messiah.

Another example, is Jesus' reaction to Peter in John 21. Jesus was walking with Peter, speaking of things that would happen to Peter in the future. Peter turned and saw John following. He asked Jesus about John. Jesus, in essence, told Peter that it was not his business (vs. 23ff). He had already told him what his business was, *"...You must follow me..."* (vs. 22ff). The honest and instructive aspects of Christ's love for Peter compelled Him to deal with Peter's problem; which was his interest in what others did or did not do or get—instead of focusing on what Jesus commanded him to do. To love honestly requires a fine balance of insight, wisdom, kindness, and courage.

f) Jesus had a "saving" kind of love. His love for others was able to save them because He was willing to make the sacrifices required. He sacrificed or laid down his life an hour at a time and a day at a time. How? By putting others' needs and interests above His own. In doing so, He lived what He taught. That is the secret of a love that changes lives (2 Corinthians 8:9 and John 4:39-42).

HOW CAN WE LOVE ONE ANOTHER AS HE LOVED?

Strangely, most of us have very little trouble loving as Jesus loved when it comes to meeting the physical needs of our sisters or brothers in Christ. When we see a need, we reach out and try to meet that need—even without being asked. We discern a need, we find out what needs to be done, we figure out how to do it, and then we do it. But this is often not the case, when our brothers/sisters needs are spiritual. We are hesitant. We are afraid to reach out to them. In fact, our most common reaction when we see a brother or sister trapped in a spiritual problem, (i.e., gossiping, slandering, lying, raging, etc., etc.) is to turn away in embarrassment. Yet the focus of our Savior's ministry was meeting the spiritual needs of men. In fact, Paul was very specific about helping one another in this particular way. In Galatians 6:1 he said, *"...Brothers, if some one is caught in a sin, you who are spiritual should restore him gently..."* And in Romans 15:14 Paul assures us that Christians have the tools to reach out and aid one another with spiritual problems for he said, *"...I myself am convinced, my brothers, that you yourselves are full of goodness, complete in knowledge and competent to instruct one another..."* So why don't we reach out to one another spiritually? Because:

1) We think it's the elders' responsibility. We might usurp their authority—that is a myth. True, the elders are responsible for reaching out to help with spiritual problems. But nowhere in the scripture does it even vaguely imply that they alone are responsible. Notice, that Galatians 6:1 and Romans 15:14 are both addressed to Christians, not

specifically to elders.

2) We're afraid we don't know enough to help with problems. This can, on occasion, be valid. But, the next question is, "How many years have you not known enough?" Ignorance is an excuse only as long as your ignorance is excusable. But after a certain time, ignorance becomes a sin. Not only because we are neglecting the study of God's Word but because we are using it to hide behind.

3) But, worst of all, we are afraid we MIGHT have a beam in our eye. Or, we could actually have a beam in our eye that is blinding us to others' spiritual needs (Matthew 7:3,4). If this is our excuse, we only have one choice. We must find out the truth. If we don't, then we must quit trying to hide behind the possibility. If we truly do have a beam in our eye, then we must get busy and remove it. But sometimes we honestly don't know if we have a beam in our eye or not. After all, all of us have known people who have problems and are not aware of it. So, just to be safe, take the Beam-In-The-Eye Test below. Then take whatever steps are necessary.

BEAM-IN-THE-EYE TEST

People with a beam in their eye usually experience a great deal of pain and conflict. They are susceptible to sin and often are numb to feelings of compassion and mercy. A beam in the eye is a very serious spiritual illness and requires immediate attention. By comparing your behavior to the beam in the eye symptoms listed below, you can determine if you are afflicted, and to what degree, and you can make plans to overcome it.

BEAM-IN-THE-EYE victims often:

—make rash statements about what someone should do in a situation when they really don't know all the facts,

—talk to others about the problem that are not involved in the problem or the solution (i.e., "Have you noticed how Jenny lies? Why don't you talk to your aunt who knows her cousin, who is married to her brother, who could talk to her mother and get her to talk to Jenny about this problem."). That is not the way God teaches us to handle a spiritual problem.

—rarely spend time checking out their own lives to see if they have the same problem.

—have not had much experience in 'overcoming' or 'working' through a problem in their own lives. Instead they tend to live comfortably with their own problems excusing them as 'weaknesses' or, the age-old rationale, 'That is just the way I am.'

—get "very angry" at the person with the problem and tend to look down on them.

—tell the offender where he is wrong but never take the time to help by searching the scripture for a solution to his problem. (This is one of the main differences between 'loving confrontation' and 'telling someone off').

IF YOUR EYES ARE BEAM FREE

After taking the beam-in-the-eye test, you may decide your vision is obstructed. In that case, develop a logical plan to overcome it. Because you cannot reach out and meet your brothers' spiritual needs if you cannot see clearly. For a beam in your eye, not only undermines the confidence others have in you, but it also distorts your vision. But if your eyes are beam free—you have a responsibility in the name of love to minister to your brothers' needs. So, ask God to help you be sensitive to your spiritual family and their needs. As a result of your prayer a sister/brother with a spiritual problem may come to your attention. If so you should:

1) Patiently observe for a little while. Don't get caught up in hasty conclusions. Jesus said in John 7:24, "...Stop judging by mere appearances, and make a right judgment..." Jesus was saying that appearances could be deceiving, that they should instead weigh and think through their evaluations. Therefore, when we notice a sister entangled in a sin (lying, gossiping, criticizing, adultery, stealing, etc.), we should take the time to observe long enough that we understand what we see and judge it properly.

2) Next, look back, have you had a similar problem? This helps in many ways. If you had a similar problem, it is helpful to remember how you felt during that time, and the things you thought, and the reactions you had. Plus you are not tempted as much to react self-righteously when you identify with their problem.

3) Now, search God's Word for a solution by command or example. This is the step that determines just how useful you will be in helping others overcome spiritual problems. It is often easy to see a problem, and want to help. And we can even generate the courage to make ourselves go talk to them about the problem. But unless we go with some type of real help, we often do more damage than good. When Jesus came to help man, he came with solutions, even left those solutions with the church in the form of the Living Word and commanded the church to love as he had loved. But we often go to a sister/brother with the right attitude and right motive, but no solution because we have not taken the time, or put in the effort to find out how God tells them to deal with their problem. The result can be:

—you only have your own wisdom to offer them, which may be inadequate, or

—they may feel there is no solution for their problem and they become entrapped in despair. Or, they try a reasonable sounding solution you have offered, but if it doesn't work, they decide you really did not know what you were talking about, so they give up. On the other hand, if they try a solution based on a scripture, and it doesn't work the first time, they will more likely try again, because they have confidence God truly knows the answers.

5) Next, accept and love the one with the problem. Begin praying for God to give you an opportunity to share with them. And if you are the best person to help your sister or brother, the opportunity will come. If it does not—then be confident that either the person is not ready to hear you yet, or perhaps, there is someone else whose words they will better understand. This does not mean you are incapable of helping others, it just means you are not the best one to help in this situation.

For example, have you ever had someone tell you something that you didn't understand? Then perhaps someone else said the same thing but in different words. All of a sudden it was perfectly clear. The first person was probably just as capable, but you understood the second. Or, have you ever heard something dozens of times and then all of a sudden one day you "really" hear it? For the first time, you understand it. So, if after you have prayed for opportunity, one doesn't come about, God is just saying, "You are not the best person to help at this time, or he/she is not ready to deal with the solution at this time" (2 Timothy 2:25,26).

Understand, that waiting for God to bring us an opportunity does not mean that we sit home and wait for our sister/brother to come to the door and say, "I have this terrible problem that I need your help in solving." Waiting for God's opportunity means reaching out in loving behavior to them (the behaviors of 1 Corinthians 13:4-7) and then watching for an opportunity to share God's solution with them.

For example, years ago when I first began to take sharing one another's burdens seriously, I would notice that certain sisters would 'be in my way' all the time. It just seemed that every time I turned around I would be about to step on one. Invariably, if I took the time to observe them for a while and prayed for insight and opportunity, the day would come that I could comfortably say to them, "Why don't we have lunch together and get to know one another better." And we would. The result was always the same, some deep and troubling problem would come out. Not every time did I have the scriptural solution on my tongue—but I could go home and find it.

73

The urgency of this kind of reaching out was made dramatically clear to me. I followed a sister (that had suddenly been getting in my way) to her car one day and asked her to have coffee. The time we spent over that cup of coffee revealed a tormented woman that was literally being eaten alive with jealousy and envy of her ex-husband's second wife. Later, she told me that on the first day I spoke to her, she had decided to go home from church, clean her house and kill herself. But the invitation for coffee and the time in God's Word together seeking solutions had turned her life around.

But loving in this way, involves hard work and commitment. If we decide we are going to reach out and lovingly confront, we must be ready to stay with them until the problem is solved. And this is not always easy. Because they may take up more time than we WANT to give, they may not try as hard to overcome as we THINK they can, they may get angry with us out of their own frustration and failure, they may NOT really be committed to overcoming the problem. But Jesus stays with us during all of these reactions. And we must be committed to staying with sisters or brothers during their times of need. Again, we see the difference between loving confrontation and 'telling off.'

5) We must pray to be God's instrument for healing their broken life instead of becoming their crutch. It is one thing to walk alongside, giving aid and support while a broken leg mends, it is quite another to walk alongside just dragging someone's broken leg. And you can easily measure your effectiveness. If when you momentarily step away from a brother/sister you have been helping, they fall flat, then you have not helped heal—you have only given temporary aid. The only way to insure healing is to take them to the real source of power. We must not make them dependent on us as their channel of power. Let them see us finding the principles and solutions for their problems in the Word. Let them hear us praying to God for help and healing in their behalf. In this way we can lead them to God, His Son, and His Spirit the real source of power.

BUT FIRST

Before we take any of the steps mentioned above, we must clothe ourselves in the garments of Galatians 6:1, Humility and Gentleness.

DISCUSSION QUESTIONS

1. What point in this chapter had the most impact on you? Why?

2. How does Romans 15:14 relate to our responsibility to reach out to one another in times of spiritual trouble?

74

3. What does being "full of goodness" involve?

4. Does it mean "perfect?" (1 John 1:8-10)

5. How can we "instruct" one another? Can you think of some scriptural examples? (What about the books of Timothy?)

Chapter Seven

The Spirit's Ministries For God's Children

Part 1
THE PROMISE

Have you known people who appear to experience more joy and enthusiasm in their Christian walk than you? Has it made you wonder if something is wrong with them? Or, even worse, is something wrong with you? Or, perhaps, you have read verses that mention the Spirit living in you and, consequently, asked yourself, "How can I tell if the Spirit is living in me?" Or, maybe, you have heard people mention the power of the Spirit in their lives and you have, for some unexplained reason, felt slightly deprived. At the same time, you wondered if you really understood what they were talking about. If you have experienced these or similar situations, you are probably ready for an in-depth study of the Holy Spirit. But first, take comfort in this thought: The spirit can fulfill His part in your redemption even if you don't understand His role. But your lack of understanding may cause you to miss many exciting, faith-building vistas. For the knowledge and awareness of the indwelling Spirit, makes your spiritual walk more exciting, and removes confusion, frustration and feebleness from your life in Jesus. Without a doubt the Spirit can play His role in our salvation without our knowledge, but it seems unlikely we could reach our spiritual potential without an informed appreciation of Him and His power. And that is the purpose of this chapter—to develop an informed appreciation of God's Holy Spirit as we reach for our Spiritual Potential.

GATHERING DATA

Any serious study must begin with accumulating all the information available from the most reliable sources. For the only real authority on the Holy Spirit is God, His Son and His Spirit, so, let's go to the Bible.

SOME INTERESTING BIBLE FACTS ABOUT THE SPIRIT

In the Bible there are approximately 259 scriptures or passages that refer to the God's Holy Spirit. Of these 259, 69 are in the Old Testament and 190 in the New Testament.

FROM THE OLD TESTAMENT WE LEARN:

• The first mention of the Holy Spirit in the Bible is in Genesis 1:2, when it speaks of His role in creation, *"...God's Spirit moved upon the face of the deep..."*

• The first time the Bible refers to the Spirit of God being in a man is when it speaks of Joseph in Genesis 41:38, *"...a man in whom the Spirit of God is..."*

• The first time we hear God say He would endow a man with 'extraordinary gifts' through the Spirit is in Exodus 31:1-5. They were gifts of craftsmanship given to be used in building the tabernacle in the wilderness.

• Isaiah and Ezekiel spoke of the Holy Spirit most frequently in the Old Testament. And most of their references involved the coming Messiah, His Kingdom, His purpose, and the Spirit's promised involvement.

FROM THE NEW TESTAMENT WE LEARN:

• The first reference to the Holy Spirit in the New Testament is in Matthew 1:18 at Jesus' conception.

• The gospels of Luke and John mention the Holy Spirit more than Matthew and Mark. In fact, Mark has only 6 references.

• The longest single passage regarding the Spirit in the New Testament is in 1 Corinthians 12, 13, 14.

• Although 1 Corinthians has the longest single passage, the Book of Acts contains the most information concerning the Holy Spirit.

• Romans the 8th chapter describes the spiritual man, Galatians 5:23 lists the fruit of the Spirit, and 1 Corinthians 12 and Romans 12 lists the gifts of the Spirit.

• The books of 2 and 3 John, and Philemon are the only books of the New Testament that make no reference to the Holy Spirit.

The above information is interesting to Bible students, but it's only statistics. And statistics can be useful when they signal the beginning of a deep study but they are useless if they become the focus of the study.

SO – LET'S GET SERIOUS

The Holy Spirit is real. He is not just a messenger or a righteous ghost. There is no difference between the term Holy Spirit and the Spirit. The adjective "holy" was usually added in translation to identify which Spirit was meant. The Spirit just like God and Christ has all the characteristics of a person. He:

* (a) has a mind - Romans 8:27
  (b) has knowledge - 1 Corinthians 2:11
  (c) has affections - Romans 15:30
  (d) makes decisions - 1 Corinthians 12:11
  (e) speaks - 1 Timothy 4:1
  (f) witnesses - John 15:26
  (g) teaches - John 14:26
  (h) guides - John 16:13
  (i) leads and forbids - Acts 16:6-10
  (j) grieves (Ephesians 4:30)
  (k) can be resisted - Acts 5:3
  (l) can be sinned against - Matthew 12:32

The Holy Spirit also has all the characteristics of God. He:

* (a) is eternal - Hebrews 9:14
  (b) is omniscient - 1 Corinthians 2:10
  (c) is omnipotent - Micah 3:8
  (d) is omnipresent - Psalm 139:7-20
  (e) creates - Psalm 104:30
  (f) regenerates man - John 3:5
  (g) will resurrect the body - Romans 8:11
  (h) gave miraculous gifts to men - 1 Corinthians 12:4-11

Jesus included the Holy Spirit in the Godhead when He told His disciples to, "...baptize...in the name of the Father, the Son and the Holy Spirit..." (Matthew 28:18-20). And He was part of Paul's famous benediction in 2 Corinthians 13:14, "Grace of Christ; Love of God; Communion of Holy Spirit." These passages help us to realize the Spirit is an individual. And He has a responsibility and a part in God's scheme to redeem man. But, this information does not reveal the most exciting aspect of the Christian's walk with the Spirit, which was first made known in a mysterious promise.

---

* Rogers, Richard, *The Holy Spirit*, chptr. 1.

THE PROMISE

God, has made, and kept, numerous promises to man since the beginning of time. But the two most gracious has been His promise of a Savior and the Spirit. *"...I will give you a new heart and put a new spirit in you;...And I will put my Spirit in you and move you to follow my decrees and be careful to keep my laws..."* (Ezekiel 36:26,27) *"...And I will pour out on the house of David and the inhabitants of Jerusalem the Spirit of grace and supplication..."* (Zechariah 12:10f). Such promises were mystifying and new to the Israelites, not because they were unfamiliar with the Spirit. For He had been active in the Old Testament. In fact, He had appeared in creation, revealed dreams, given prophetic visions, empowered the rulers of Israel, given gifts of craftsmanship and even dwelt "with" them. But "The Promise" was something entirely different. This was part of the great mystery that had been hidden through the ages. It was a portion of the prophecies that the prophets themselves, and the angels in heaven, had not understood—and longed to look into (1 Peter 1:10-12). It was a portion of the mystery Paul spoke of in Colossians 1:26,27, *"...the mystery that has been kept hidden for ages and generations, but is now disclosed to the saints. To them God has chosen to make known among the Gentiles the glorious riches of this mystery, which is Christ in you, the hope of glory..."* The mystery was not only that the gospel would be offered to the Gentiles. But that Christ would be "in" His followers. Christ, Himself, repeated this portion of the promise in John 7:38,39 when He said, *"Whoever believes in me, as the Scripture has said, streams of living water will flow from within him."* By this he meant the Spirit, whom those who believed in him were later to receive. Up to that time the Spirit had not been given, since Jesus had not yet been glorified.

This does not mean that the disciples had not participated in the power of the Spirit before this time, because they had. Jesus had already sent them out to preach, He had given them power to perform miracles, heal the sick, and cast out demons. But after His glorification the Spirit was to come and be IN them. John 14:16-18 expands on this difference, *"...And I will ask the Father, and he will give you another Counselor to be with you forever—the Spirit of truth. The world cannot accept him, because it neither sees him nor knows him. But you know him, for he lives WITH you and will be IN you..."* The Spirit did come, as Christ had promised. He came on the first Pentecost after Jesus was glorified. And on that occasion Peter stood up, with the eleven and declared to the Jews that the promise of the Spirit was being fulfilled, *"...this is what was spoken by the prophet Joel:*

'In the last days, God says, I will pour out my Spirit on all people...' "
(Acts 2:17f). Not only did he tell the thousands of Jews listening to
him they were witnessing the fulfillment of Joel's prophecy, he also
told them they could receive this same Spirit, *"...Repent and be bap-*
tized, every one of you, in the name of Jesus Christ so that your sins
may be forgiven. And you will receive the gift of the Holy Spirit. The
promise is for you and your children and for all who are far off—for
all whom the Lord our God will call..." (Acts 2:38,39). Peter mentioned this gift again in Acts 5:32 when he said, *"...And we (the Apos-*
tles) are witnesses of these things; and so is the Holy Spirit, whom God
hath given to them that obey him..."

BUT WHAT DOES IT MEAN?

It means that when a person becomes a Christian he receives the
Holy Spirit, who has a very convenient aspect. He is not limited to
flesh and blood reality; he is of another dimension. And in that dimension (the spirit world) he can actually take up residence in our
bodies. According to Paul that is what he does, *"...Don't you know*
that you yourselves are God's temple and that God's Spirit lives in
you?..." and *"...Do you not know that your body is a temple of the*
Holy Spirit, who is in you, who you have received from God..."
(1 Corinthians 3:16; 6:19).

And in these two verses we glimpse another remarkable wonder.
A situation that is beyond the scope of our limited thinking. But stated
in the Word so conclusively, that believers cannot deny it. For the
Word does not attempt to explain it—it just states it as fact.

**(1) *"...he that abideth in love abideth in God, and God abideth*
in him..." (1 John 4:11-16). This passage, along with 1 Corinthians
3:16; 6:16; Philippians 2:13; and 2 Thessalonians 1:1, says: **Chris-**
tians abide in God and God abides in Christians.

(2) *"If any man is in Christ, he is a new creation..."* (Galatians
2:20) These and a multitude of other passages say: **Christians are**
in Christ and Christ is in Christians.

(3) *"...The Spirit dwelleth in you..."* (Romans 8:11) *"...Walk in*
the Spirit..." (Galatians 5:16) (AV) These verses and others say: **The**
Spirit is in Christians and Christians are in the Spirit. All of
these passages describe **one condition, the same condition, the**
saved condition.

And the New Testament uses these designations (God in Christians,

---

** Coffman, Burton, *Commentary on Galatians, Ephesians, Philip-*
pians, Colossians.

Christians in God; Christ in Christians, Christians in Christ; The Spirit in Christians, Christians in the Spirit) interchangeably time and time again. For this reason, we will use the power of God, the power of Christ andthe power of the Spirit interchangeably because in their perfect unity it is impossible to separate The Three that are One.

But God was being more than gracious when He sent the Spirit to live within us. He had a purpose, and that purpose was to DO for man what man could NOT do for himself. And the things man cannot do for himself comprise a 4-Fold Ministry for the Spirit: The Ministry of Certification; The Helping Ministry; The Ministry of Practical Power; and The Ministry of Partnership.

The Spirit's Ministries For God's Children

Part 2
MINISTRY OF CERTIFICATION AND HELP

THE SPIRIT IS A SEAL
AND EARNEST FOR CHRISTIANS

SEAL—The Spirit seals us for the day of salvation. In other words, being given the Holy Spirit is like being stamped on the forehead, "This human being belongs to God." For that is what a seal is: a mark impressed on an object denoting authenticity, a stamp that confirms, etc. A seal on a document identifies it as the real thing, certifying it is not counterfeit. It also gives it legal standing. Since we are sealed, we are certified authentic followers of Jesus Christ. (To be a certified follower of Jesus has more potential than having a Ph.D.)

AN EARNEST—Paul describes this particular role of the Spirit in three verses: *"...Who (God) also sealed us and gave us the earnest of the Spirit in our hearts...Now he that wrought us for this very thing is God, who gave us the earnest of the Spirit...Which (the Spirit) is an earnest of our inheritance, unto the redemption of God's own possession, unto the praise of His glory..."* (2 Corinthians 1:22; 5:5; Ephesians 1:14) In other words, God has deposited His Spirit in our hearts for right now as a guarantee that we will one day receive the balance of our inheritance. Put simply, the Spirit is a down payment from God to us toward the coming glories of heaven. (That is a better future than mutual funds.)

The Spirit ministers to us in these two roles automatically, without our knowledge or awareness, in fact, His very presence is our seal and our earnest.

HE SANCTIFIES US

The Spirit also sanctifies us. To sanctify means to dedicate or bring to holiness. And it is overwhelming to realize that living within us is a power that has dedicated us (or separated us apart for God) and is now focusing on bringing us to holiness. In 2 Thessalonians 2:13,14, *"...But we ought always to thank God for you, brothers loved by the Lord, because from the beginning God chose you to be saved through the sanctifying work of the Spirit through our gospel, that you might share in the glory of our Lord Jesus Christ..."* Sanctification is another way the Spirit ministers to us. From the moment He takes up his abode in our hearts, He is committed to sanctifying us. And His mere presence does that by declaring we are set aside for God. But sanctification also includes "bringing to holiness." And the Spirit is dedicated to that assignment. And we will discuss this aspect of His sanctifying ministry in The Ministry of Partnership.

HE HELPS US

One of the names for the Holy Spirit is Comforter. And that is the role He fulfills in his Helping Ministry for Christians. Within the scope of that ministry, one of the most considerate, supportive and loving is His comfort of intercession. We are all familiar with Romans 8:26,27 which says, *"...In the same way, the Spirit helps us in our weakness. We do not know what we ought to pray, but the Spirit himself intercedes for us with groans that words cannot express..."* This verse begins with a reference to the preceding scriptures, *"...In the same way..."* therefore, it is important to consider the previous discussion to put these statements in perspective.

In chapter 7 and in chapter 8, Paul discusses the dilemma Christians struggle with: they are new creations with the Spirit of God living in them, but they are imprisoned in a "body of death" and the result is conflict and weakness. This weakness is expressed through groanings toward the coming glorification. In these chapters he mentions three areas of groanings: (1) the groaning of creation; (2) the groaning of God's children, and (3) the groaning of the Spirit in the children's behalf. And in verse 26, he says that when the weaknesses Christians struggle with reaches our very prayer life and we are so helpless and confused we do not even know how to pray, the Spirit is there interceding for us with groanings or yearnings or sighs that words cannot express.

Then in verse 27 Paul explains further. We are told that as God searches the heart He understands the mind of the Spirit, and consequently those groanings or yearnings or sighs become prayer requests to Him. In these situations, the Spirit is more than an interpreter for us. Because not only can He translate our groans into words, He can translate our needs into words, when we can't.

In fact, we could compare the condition described in verse 26 to being stricken with a weakness that has not only paralyzed our ability to act, it has also paralyzed our ability to think, understand and express our needs. Then visualize a ministering angel coming to our aid. An angel who not only understands our weakness but also can see its solution. And that ministering angel takes over for us expressing those needs to a loving and merciful God.

HE RECEIVES GOD'S LOVE
INTO OUR HEARTS

We are told in Romans 5:5, *"...And hope does not disappoint us, because God has poured out his love into our hearts by the Holy Spirit, whom he has given us..."* This is a beautiful service the Spirit performs for God's children. From reading this scripture in the context of the passage, Romans 5:1-11, we can see that: (1) NO matter how difficult the trials we face, we can rejoice. Because through our trials, we develop the qualities needed to produce character which gives birth to hope. (2) And hope in God will not disappoint us, embarrass us or shame us. In fact, such hope is logical, because God has already proven His faithfulness, dependability and love. He did this by the great outpouring of His love—over us (through the blood of Christ)—around us (through His loving care)—and into us (through His Holy Spirit). And that same Spirit continues to live within us reminding us of God's love and producing the fruit of the Spirit, one of which is 'love'.

The love God pours into our hearts is His divine love. It is not like the love mankind typically displays. Jesus points this out in Luke 6:32 saying in essence that—man, by nature, wants to do to other men what other men do to him. For example, we love those who love us, we loan only to those who will return, we do good deeds for those who do good deeds for us, etc., etc. But God's love is willing to love those who do not deserve it, do good deeds for those who have never done a good deed for Him and loan to men who don't repay. That's divine love. The seed of this love is in our hearts because God has poured it there. And His Holy Spirit receives it and nurtures it into the full grown 'fruit of love.'

THE SPIRIT IS WAITING
TO RESURRECT US

When Paul wanted to emphasize the might of God's power that is working in us, he pointed out it was the same power used to resurrect Christ (Ephesians 1:21). *"...and his incomparably great power for us who believe. That power is like the working of his mighty strength, which he exerted in Christ when he raised him from the dead..."* Power like that is beyond our comprehension but not beyond our experience because the mighty strength God exerted in Jesus, He will exert in us. In fact, that power is living within us now. *"...And if the Spirit of him who raised Jesus from the dead is living in you, he who*

85

raised Christ from the dead will also give life to your mortal bodies through his Spirit, who lives in you..." Not only is this promise exciting but faith in it can free us from the fear of death that Satan has used to enslave us. Because in Christ, death is just a portal between our earthly pilgrimage and our eternal home in heaven. And the channel for our resurrection, God's Holy Spirit, already lives within us.

DISCUSSION QUESTIONS

1. What point in the 'Gathering Data' portion of this lesson had the most impact on you? Why?

2. What point in the 'Ministry of Certification' had the most impact on you? Why?

3. What point in the 'Ministry of Helping' had the most impact on you? Why?

(Have each person in the group verbalize the answer to at least one of these questions—better yet, all three.)

The Spirit's Ministries
For God's Children

Part 3
MINISTRY OF PRACTICAL POWER

THE SPIRIT ENABLES, EMPOWERS,
AND STRENGTHENS

Ephesians 3:16, along with Ephesians 1:19; 3:20 and Romans 15:13 refer to the power available to Christians, *"...I pray that out of his glorious riches he may strengthen you with power through his Spirit in your inner being..."* But, unfortunately, two typical reactions often void this VERY REAL POWER in our lives: (1) One reaction is to read the scriptures relating to the Spirit's ability to empower us, mentally acknowledge them, philosophically discuss them, verbally teach them, and then promptly ignore them. This reaction is comfortable. It does not challenge our study, our growth, or our understanding. It is similar to the reaction of the one-talent man...and God called him wicked and lazy (Matthew 25:26). (2) A second reaction is to treat it as a magic charm that mysteriously relieves us of all responsibility for exercising discipline or self-control, exerting effort, or "striving" to be what God wants us to be. Instead, this reaction teaches, "Just get out of the way and let the Spirit do it for you—you can't rely on yourself." Sadly, there is just enough truth in this statement to make it deceiving. In our push-button age, this second concept has a great deal of appeal. But, it ignores Paul's discussion in Romans 7:7-25 regarding the struggle with sin all of us have. It does not explain Paul's reference to beating his body daily into submission (1 Corinthians 9:24-27). And it is incompatible with Philippians 3:12-14 where Paul speaks of "straining" and "pressing" on toward the goal.

These responses often come from sincere Christians. Christians who are searching to understand the Holy Spirit's role. But neither response conforms to Biblical teaching and neither response can be practically applied to our daily Christian walk.

The Spirit's Ministries
For God's Children

Part 4
MINISTRY OF PRACTICAL POWER

THE SPIRIT'S POWER IS PRACTICAL

To make the Spirit's power practical in our lives, we must understand why it was given. And a study of WHY not only enlightens, it also surprises. For the New Testament reveals a variety of purposes for the Spirit's power in our lives. To begin with:

THE PRACTICAL POWER TO HOPE

This is an unexpected power the Spirit exercises in our behalf. And one we rarely hear mentioned. Paul speaks of it in Romans 15:13, *"...May the God of hope fill you with great joy and peace as you trust in him, so that you may overflow with hope by the power of the Holy Spirit..."* But why should we need the power of the Holy Spirit to hope? Because, even though we are more than conquerors, we are still human. We are subject to the disappointments, failures, and weaknesses of humanity. Therefore, losing hope is a great temptation—one God cannot afford for us to succumb to. Because without hope, man perishes. And since God has not yet replaced our humanity with glorification, He gives us His Spirit to empower our hope-ability.

In John 16:33, we can see that Jesus was very aware of this human condition when He said to His disciples, *"...I have told you these things, so that in me you may have peace. In this world you will have trouble. But take heart! I have overcome the world..."* In this scripture Jesus is offering them a hope that will give them peace. For He is explaining that since they have been warned of His approaching death, they can have peace when it happens. Because they will know everything is going according to God's plan. And the confidence that God is in control gives birth to hope. And after hope is born, then the Spirit empowers Christians to live and walk in it. This makes no sense to the world, because they do not have the power of the Spirit in their lives enabling them to live in hope during times of victory and times of trouble. For only, *"...those who wait (which implies trusting faith) for the Lord will gain new strength; They will mount up with wings like eagles, They will run and not get tired, They will walk and not become weary..."* (Isaiah 40:31).

THE PRACTICAL POWER
TO FULFILL AND COMPLETE

This facet of the Spirit's power in our lives is one of the most exciting. Not just because of what it does, but because of what it teaches us to do. Scripture teaches that God's power is real and at work in us (Ephesians 1:19; 3:16). But often, our Christian walk is not traveled in power, instead we drag along in fear and defeat. And the major reason is, we haven't mastered the formula that implements the power of God. But thanks to Paul, and the Spirit who inspired him, 1 Thessalonians 1:11 gives us insight into that formula for power, *"...With this in mind, we constantly pray for you, that our God may count you worthy of his calling, and that by his power he may fulfill every good purpose of yours and every act prompted by your faith."* Do you see the formula? It is (A + B + T) or ASKING + BELIEVING + TRUSTING which are the sum total of faith, plain and simple. Something we have all heard many, many times. But if we are not traveling in God's power, we have not heard it enough.

Because belief and trust will motivate us to step out for the Lord and depend on God's power to help us complete. Look at the scripture again, *"...by his power he may fulfill every good purpose of yours and every act prompted by your faith..."* Peter displayed this kind of faith in Matthew 14:28-32. Jesus came to them walking on water. And Peter said, *"...Lord if it is you...tell me to come to you on the water..."* (ASKING). Jesus answered, "come," and Peter stepped out of the boat (BELIEVING AND TRUSTING). And he actually walked on water. From the time Jesus said, "come" the power was available. But it was not empowering Peter until he took the first step out of the boat trusting Jesus to empower him to walk on water. Then he started the next step and the power was there to complete it, and the next step and the next step. Each step he started he received power to complete. While in the boat he had not been zapped with 'all' the power he needed—even for a small journey across the water to Jesus (We can know this by what we see happen later.) He was only given the power to complete each step he started in faith and trust. That is the way God insists we walk in faith. We must start each step, and He empowers us to complete it. Then we must start the next. And on and on it goes—walking by faith every step of the way.

But Peter, foolishly, took his eyes off Jesus (his source of faith and power) and saw the wind and the waves and was overwhelmed by fear (a source of defeat because fear destroys trust). From this, we can draw 3 conclusions: (a) ask for God's help—Peter asked Jesus to let him walk on water, (2) if the answer is 'yes' step out in faith, and (3) don't lose sight of Jesus—for He is our source of faith and without faith we can't spiritually walk on water or anything else. But if we ask God's bidding, then step out in faith to teach a class, lead a Bible study, develop a hospital or prison ministry, etc., etc., we will be given the power to complete each good purpose.

But without the power of the Spirit in our daily Christian walk, we will have to depend totally on our own strength, our own endurance, our own ingenuity, and our own ability. Sadly, many sincere Christians are relying on nothing more than these human tools today. And the result is tired, frustrated brothers and sisters. Tired because they are putting in long hours trying to pull something together without seeking God's help, and frustrated because they try so hard and nothing seems to work. But we don't have to live like that for within us lives the Spirit who has power to fulfill every good purpose. Every good purpose THAT IS ACCORDING TO GOD'S WILL—for sometimes the Spirit forbids some of our chosen purposes (Acts 16:6,7).

But if, the Holy Spirit is going to forbid our involvement; we can be confident, He will make it plain. And He makes it plain by closing or opening doors and presenting or removing opportunities. And if the door is opened and the opportunity is there, you can be confident you will be empowered to fulfill it. (A personal example. A few years ago, I was invited to lecture at a major Christian University in Texas at their annual lectureship. It was a very great honor and I looked forward to it with excitement. But right before the Lectureship I became ill. But with determination, we went on praying fervently I would be well when it came time for my sessions. But I wasn't, in fact, I was worse I didn't know what to do. Finally, my husband and I decided that since God had not removed the opportunity, He would empower me to fulfill it.

So, a chair was placed on the stage and I was seated with a forced smile and a lapel microphone, feeling terrible. But, the minute I was introduced, I perked up and lecturing from the chair I did fine. But as soon as my lecture was over I had to be driven back to our motel. Where I stayed in bed until the next session. This went on for three days, and the remarkable thing was—I did great—as long as I was lecturing. (In fact, if my fever had not been so high, I would have thought it was all psychosomatic.)

That spring I was committed to nine other retreats, seminars, workshops, etc. And I was ill all spring—except when I was lecturing at seminars, workshops, etc. This sounds brave and self-sacrificing but it wasn't. Neither was I being a martyr nor foolhardy. On the contrary, I was ministering to myself as well as to other Christians. Because the only times I felt good that entire spring was during the times I shared God's Word with His women. Which was nothing more than stepping out in faith to meet His opportunities.

Another scripture that speaks of available power in a very similar way is 1 Peter 4:11, *"...if anyone serves, he should do it with the strength God provides..."* The word translated strength here is often translated, "power." But regardless of whether the word is translated strength or power, it is making the same point—the strength or power to serve or fulfill every good purpose comes from God through His Spirit (Ephesians 3:16). So we can plainly see the power of the Spirit is not a philosophy without substance nor a fantasy without practical application. The power of the Spirit is very real and is available to us as we Reach for our Spiritual Potential.

THE PRACTICAL POWER TO OVERCOME

This function of the Spirit's power in our lives is closely related to the power to fulfill or complete. Because, if we would overcome Satan's snares, we must not only resist temptation but we must also step out and fulfill God's will for us. Second Timothy 3:1-5 is a good example of people who were not using God's power to overcome, *"...There will be terrible times in the last days. People will be lovers of themselves, lovers of money, boastful, proud, abusive, disobedient to their parents, ungrateful, unholy, without love, unforgiving, slanderous, without self-control, brutal, not lovers of the good, treacherous, rash, conceited, lovers of pleasure rather than lovers of God— having a form of godliness but denying its power. Have nothing to do with them..."* In the latter part of this passage, we are told, these people have, *"...a form of godliness but deny its power..."* The power these people were denying was the power to live a life of holiness. The same life Jesus lived, and the life Paul spoke of when he said, *"...follow me as I follow Christ..."* We have the power to follow Jesus so we don't have to follow the patterns of the world. Paul reinforces this point in Romans 12:2, *"Do not conform any longer to the patterns of the world, but be transformed."* And anytime we don't live a transformed life we are denying God's power to change us.

But, sometimes, it is not the patterns of the world that cause us to deny God's power. Rather it is our self-indulgence or ignorance that causes us to say, "Well, that is just the way I am; our whole family is that way; we have always had high tempers and there is nothing we can do about it."

In these (all too frequent) situations, we are not only denying the power the Spirit provides for us to overcome, we are also grieving Him. Notice in Ephesians, 4:29-32, *"...Do not let any unwholesome talk come out of your mouths, but only what is helpful for building others up according to their needs, that it may benefit those who*

91

listen, And do not grieve the Holy Spirit of God, with whom you were sealed for the day of redemption. Get rid of all bitterness, rage and anger, brawling and slander, along with every form of malice. Be kind and compassionate to one another, forgiving each other, just as in Christ God forgave you..." Ephesians 4:17-5:21 has become known as a major behavior modification passage of the Bible. In it Paul is simply telling the Ephesians to QUIT doing what is wrong by DOING what is right. And in the middle of this discussion he says, *"...don't grieve the Holy Spirit of God..."* By this he meant: don't grieve the Holy Spirit by neglecting to replace the wrong behaviors with the right behaviors. Some versions of that passage say, *"...don't frustrate the Holy Spirit..."* The two words together probably express what the Spirit feels; as He watches us let sin rule our lives when His power is available to overcome.

The formula for this power is (B + D + T) which means BELIEVE + DECIDE + TRUST = POWER. For example, in Ephesians 4 we are told to replace lying with speaking the truth. To do so, we must first BELIEVE God's Word when it says we can replace lying by speaking the truth. Second, we must DECIDE to close our mouths when a lie starts to form (lightning fast sometimes) on our tongues and third, we must open our mouths TRUSTING the Spirit to empower us to speak the truth.

Or, when we lose control and are tempted to yell out in anger, we must BELIEVE what God's Word teaches about dealing with anger, we must DECIDE to close our mouths, we must TRUST the Spirit to give us power to exercise self-control and deal with the problem in God's way.

When we are tempted to criticize, gripe and complain about a brother or sister who has, or is, irritating us, we must BELIEVE God's teachings about complaining and criticizing, we must DECIDE to close our mouths on that complaint, and we must TRUST the Spirit to empower us to say something good or say nothing at all. (Is it possible that many Christians never even get to the BELIEVING part because they do not spend enough time in the Word to know what it teaches on such subjects?)

Without the power the Spirit adds to our lives, we could not consistently live a life of overcoming. We would have a few successes, a lot of failures, a few more successes and a lot more failures, and on and on it would go. Because we would have to rely on our own sense of fairness, our own unselfishness, our own discipline, and our own self-control. And our resources just couldn't meet the demand.

Therefore, God does not ask us to do what we cannot do—unless He is going to make up the difference. If He asks us to be kind, He is going to enable us to be kind. If He asks us to tell the truth, He is going to enable us to tell the truth. BUT, we must ASK then BELIEVE His Word on the subject, DECIDE to yield to His leading and TRUSTINGLY act on that decision. The result will be the power to overcome.

THE POWER TO OVERCOME CIRCUMSTANCES

One comfort the Spirit has for Christians is the power to overcome circumstances. We hear Paul teach this in his epistles, and we see him live it in his life. He writes in Romans 12:7-10, *"...To keep me from becoming conceited because of these surpassingly great revelations, there was given me a thorn in my flesh, a messenger of Satan, to torment me. Three times I pleaded with the Lord to take it away from me. But he said to me, 'My grace is sufficient for you, for my power is made perfect in weakness.' Therefore, I will boast all the more gladly about my weaknesses, so that Christ's power may rest on me. That is why, for Christ's sake, I delight in weaknesses, in insults, in hardships, in persecutions, in difficulties. For when I am weak, then I am strong..."* This passage overflows with encouragement about the power available to us. First, notice the variety of circumstances Paul refers to, "weaknesses, insults, hardships, persecutions, difficulties." That takes in every imaginable situation. He points out that when he is too weak to deal with these circumstances, then God's power is set in motion. Consequently, he becomes stronger in his weakness than he was in his own strength.

Most Christians would not deny they have experienced this remarkable power during times of hardship, i.e., the death of a loved one, overwhelming financial pressures, unresolvable health problems, etc., etc. For we all can look back on situations and circumstances that seem impossible. And from this perspective, we are astonished that we got through them. And even more astonishing, we don't even remember it being that difficult at the time.

An example—A Christian couple once had three young women living in their home going through the pain and trauma of divorce. The couple also had two teenage daughters and a toddler. All were living in a four-bedroom house, where the space and money were equally cramped. Yet, the home had a cheerful atmosphere. The love for one another and for the Lord was obviously present. So much so, that many others were constantly there sharing food and fellowship.

When the situation began developing, this couple had been dismayed. They wondered how they could possibly deal with it. So, they sought God's help, and within His boundaries, they looked at every option available. When they could find no other way, they welcomed the young women into their home. And were determined that with God's help they could cope. So with God's Word as a daily guide, the consistent practice of thankfulness, and the double doses of love, they dealt with the situation. The result was ample power to fulfill that good purpose. This example illustrates what Paul was talking about—the strength to overcome the circumstance whether it be weaknesses, hardships, insults, difficulties, persecutions, etc.

Paul needed this lesson. For by his nature, discipline and training he was a strong individual. But God planned for Paul to be even stronger. Not by exhorting him to be tougher, but by allowing him to be subjected to weaknesses. And as Paul pleaded to be delivered, God assured him, *"...my grace is sufficient for you, for my power is made perfect in weakness."* (Not that God is opposed to Christians being strong, disciplined, and dedicated. On the contrary, Timothy was admonished to be exactly that throughout 1 and 2 Timothy.) But Paul's strength must have been a hindrance to God's plan for him. Because God did not remove Paul's thorn in the flesh, but He gave him insight into its purposes: (1) it was keeping him from becoming conceited, (2) it was teaching him God's grace was all he needed to deal with any situation, and (3) it was teaching him to appreciate weaknesses and hardships; aware Christ's power in him was greater during those times. This passage does not teach that God wants us to be weak and feeble—it teaches just the opposite. God wants us to live a victorious Christian life by giving the best we have to give (even in a weakened condition) then depending and trusting in His power to make up the difference.

Here is a power formula that we can use to overcome circumstances as Paul did: (C + A + D + A + T) = POWER TO OVERCOME. Translated into the Christian language it means: (1) CONSIDER the available options and God's will concerning them; (2) ASK God for His help and wisdom; (3) DECIDE which options to pursue; (4) ACT on that decision; and (5) TRUST in God, not only for the Spirit's power, but for the conclusion. Many times we follow this formula all the way through step 4 into the first half of step 5, then we fall flat into frustration and guilt. Frustration because we don't overcome instantly and guilt because it must be our fault. So we run faster, try harder and fall deeper.

We can see an example of this in the book of Acts. Paul was delivered from dangers and imprisonments time and time again. But the imprisonment that began in Acts 21:27-36, he was not delivered from, though he asked in faith. (He also had everyone else he could write to asking in faith.) But God withheld his deliverance. There had been times God's purposes were served better with Paul out of prison. But not this time. God's purpose was being served better with Paul in prison. (Do you think Paul would have written all those letters, that became a large portion of the New Testament, if he had not been locked up?)

But Paul did not succumb to frustration and guilt when his imprisonment continued. Because he successfully completed step 5. He truly TRUSTED God. He trusted Him enough to accept God's answer to Paul's PERSISTENT prayer for delivery. And because he trusted God we hear him saying in Philippians 1:12-20, *"...Now I want you to know, brothers, that what has happened to me has really served to advance the gospel...The important thing is...Christ is preached...with your prayers and the HELP GIVEN BY THE SPIRIT OF JESUS CHRIST, what has happened to me will turn out for my deliverance...whether by LIFE or by DEATH..."*

God did eventually deliver Paul from jail and from his chains through death, a possibility Paul wrote of in Philippians 1:18-26 and one that had certain appeal to him. Until that time, God's sufficient grace and power had been delivering him with contentment. Look at Philippians 4:12,13, *"...I know what it is to be in need, and I know what it is to have plenty. I have learned the secret of being content in any and every situation, whether well fed or hungry, whether living in plenty or in want. I CAN DO EVERYTHING THROUGH HIM WHO GIVES ME STRENGTH..."* This is not weakness—this is power, REAL power.

This is how Christ overcame His fear of the cross. He considered His options and asked for God's help (John 12:27,28; Matthew 26:36-39). He came to a decision and acted on it (John 12:28; Matthew 26:45,46). He trusted His Father, realizing God was in control (John 19:11). In addition, He submitted to God's teachings in the situation. He showed compassion to the thief, He asked God to forgive His killers, He comforted Mary, and He turned to God in His agony. And He was given a glorious victory over death in His resurrection through the power of God's Holy Spirit. But victory was not new to Jesus. He had already overcome the circumstances of His life. In John 16:33, He said, *"...But take heart! I have overcome the world..."* He was not talking about the cross because, at that time, He had not died. Instead, He had been living the life of a man. He had enjoyed many of its pleasures (fellowship in the homes of friends, wedding celebrations, the love of family, the beauty of creation, the love of children). He had been delivered from threatening crowds time and again, He had experienced the power of the Spirit in His life (Luke 4).

He had also dealt with many of life's difficulties (persecutions, ridicule, distress, frustrations and temptation). But none of these circumstances had prevented Him from completing His ministry. So to His disciples He could confidently say, *"...Take heart! For I have overcome the world..."* implying His power could do the same for His followers. And to God He could say, *"...I have brought you glory on earth by completing the work you gave me to do..."*

THE PRACTICAL POWER TO GLORIFY GOD

Empowering man serves God's purposes in two ways. First, it enables His creation to live out His vision for them. Second, the victories His children experience bring glory to Him as they live and walk in faith. But, sadly, Christians sometimes try to live in a faith of their own choosing, instead of a faith based on knowledge of God's will.

For instance, there were two brothers in a little rural community. They had a beautiful farm that they worked 16 hours a day, 7 days a week—until they "got" religion. They stopped working their farm, proclaiming loudly in faith, they were 'leaving all' to do the Lord's work; and He would do theirs by finishing their crop. The result was: the crops were taken over by weeds. And both (weeds and crops) withered from lack of water. In the fall there was nothing to harvest.

What was supposed to be an act of faith to bring glory to God, only brought ridicule from non-believers, and shame for believers. In the brothers' excitement to serve God, they had not sought God's will for their lives in prayer and in His Word. Instead, they had decided what they would do for God and what God would do for them. They were living faith, but it was a faith of their own making, not faith as God teaches in His Word. God had the power to fulfill every good purpose the brothers had. For a God who parts the Red Sea could certainly preserve a crop. And He has called men before from the fields to follow Him. But these actions were according to His plan for man, not man's plan for Him. We must stay close to God in His Word, in prayer, and in the communion of the Holy Spirit. Otherwise, we can so easily be misled, mistaking OUR plan to glorify God for HIS.

And to bring glory to God is the ultimate purpose for His power in our lives just as in the life of Jesus. Listen to Paul in 2 Thessalonians 1:11-12, *"...and that by his power he may fulfill every good purpose of yours and every act prompted by your faith. We pray this SO THAT THE NAME OF OUR LORD JESUS MAY BE GLORIFIED IN YOU, and you in him, according to the grace of our God and the Lord Jesus Christ."* In 2 Corinthians 4:7 he says that our very fragileness is designed to make God's power more evident, *"...But we have this treasure (referring to their ministry) in jars of clay to SHOW THAT THIS ALL-SURPASSING POWER IS FROM GOD and not from us."* Peter also mentions this purpose in 1 Peter 4:11, *"...If any-*

one serves, he should do it with the strength God provides, *SO THAT IN ALL THINGS GOD MAY BE PRAISED THROUGH Jesus Christ. To him be the glory and the power for ever and ever. Amen...*"

THE PRACTICAL POWER TO TESTIFY

To testify, or witness, our belief in Jesus only 'sounds' simple. In reality it is often very difficult. And God knew it would be. So, in His mercy He has made His power available to us—to fill the gap between (1) what man 'can' do, and (2) what man 'must' do. For owning Jesus is a must in our salvation. In Matthew 10:32,33, "...*Whoever acknowledges me before men, I will acknowledge him before my Father in heaven. But whoever disowns me before men, I will disown him before my Father in heaven...*"

There are two ways to acknowledge Jesus before men—one is in what we say and the other is in what we do. And both count! For if we say we believe in Jesus yet our actions deny it, we have shamed our Lord. And if our actions are admirable but no one knows of our faith, then we are praised as a "nice guy" without awareness for the REAL "why" and the "how". In such cases, the world sees us as living proof that man does not need God to have it all together. Fear to witness our faith due to shyness, embarrassment or intimidation is not just a contemporary problem. Paul continually asked Christians to pray that he could speak the truth boldly. And, after the expressions of affection in his letter to Timothy, the very first thing he exhorted Timothy to do was to testify. He not only told Timothy to testify but in his exhortation to do so he disclosed a power formula for activating that power to speak out.

He started his admonition to the young Timothy with a truth, "...*God did not give us a spirit of timidity (fear), but a spirit of power, of love and self-discipline...*" Remember, the universal principle in John 8:32, "...*ye shall know the truth and the truth shall set you free...*" Well the truth Paul taught to free Timothy was—fear or timidity is not from God, therefore, it must be from the natural man or Satan. Part 2 of that truth was—POWER and LOVE and SELF-CONTROL are the spirit that God gives us. Paul is pointing out to Timothy that he has been given three of the most powerful forces known to man: (1) God's POWER, which can enable us to do anything within God's will, (2) LOVE, which is so mighty, it has enabled mothers to lift cars off trapped children, or allowed men to overcome their instincts of self-preservation and lay down their lives for others, and (3) SELF-DISCIPLINE, the force that makes frightened soldiers leave protected areas, exposing their lives to danger at a captain's command.

A second truth that Paul always focused on and taught Timothy

97

was the power of purpose, *"...join with me in suffering for the gospel by the power of God..."* By reminding him of the 'purpose' of testifying and the power available to fulfill that good purpose, he directs Timothy's focus away from fear and toward purpose and power.

He concludes by sharing another powerful truth with Timothy by reminding him they enjoy the salvation that comes with the gospel, but not because they deserve it but because Christ provided it. And he finally completes the formula by exhorting him, *"...So do not be ashamed to testify..."* That is the step into perspective—do not be ashamed.

Thus the formula for activating God's power in your life to testify is $(T(3)^2 + P)^5$ = GOD'S POWER or (Three of God's Truths kept in the proper perspective). Translated into practical Christian living it simply means: (a) FACE REALITY ABOUT THE SITUATION (truth). What are we afraid of? Whatever the fears, they are not from God. And we have within us three tools to overcome any fear and any situation— power, love and self-discipline. (b) REMEMBER OUR PURPOSE (the gospel). If we lose sight of purpose, we become disoriented. Then we have difficulty determining where to go, when to go and how to go. Consequently, we go nowhere, but in circles. But we can overcome disorientation by continually focusing on our purpose. (c) REMEMBER OUR SALVATION. Someone overcame their hesitancy, timidity or fear to share the gospel with us, otherwise, we would still be unsaved. (d) THE POWER OF PERSPECTIVE. A true and realistic perspective allows us to be proud of our faith in Jesus, not ashamed. After all, who are these people who have us intimidated? How important is their opinion of us compared to God's opinion of us? What have they done for us in comparison to what Christ has done for us?

In the past, I have occasionally found myself on planes, in airports, in department stores, in restaurants, talking to a salesman, or an acquaintance, etc., etc., and an unexpected opportunity to share my faith would sneak up on me. I would find myself vaguely embarrassed and sharing my faith in an almost apologetic manner. The result was an uncomfortable and awkward atmosphere, with me struggling inwardly with shame and guilt for my lack of boldness. Eventually I learned, that when these unexpected opportunities appeared, if I took a deep breath (silently asked for God's help) I could plunge in boldly and confidently. And I discovered that the minute I opened my mouth IN BOLDNESS the power to fulfill was there and I could continue to share my faith truthfully, sincerely and with conviction. The result was an atmosphere of interest, and respect.

THE PRACTICAL POWER
TO ENDURE AND BE PATIENT
WITH ALL JOY

In Colossians 1:9-12, Paul speaks of his prayers for the Colossians. And among his requests he mentions, *"...(We pray) that you may be invigorated and strengthened with all power, according to the might of His glory, (to exercise) every kind of endurance and patience (perseverance and forbearance) with joy..."* (Amplified). And the source that implements that power in our lives is the Spirit that lives within us. The first blessing he asks for in this passage (endurance) is the "hanging-in-there" power available to us in all circumstances. And the only thing that can interrupt its flow into our lives is our decision to give up. For as long as we are "willing" so is God's power. God has had to repeat this message to man again and again. In fact, that is what the book of Hebrews is saying, "stay with it, don't give up now, look at the advantages you have, you can make it."

Many, many passages in the New Testament say the same thing, because man has always needed to hear it. No matter what the circumstances, we overcome if we are willing to endure. Even if the circumstance literally 'kills' us. Think of Christ on the cross, He died, but He overcame. Think of the early Christian martyrs, they died but they died victorious, with their faith intact. Think of Stephen, he died at the hands of the Jews, but he died in victory, his faith was intact. Think about our own lives, we all remember difficult times we have endured. Times that we ALMOST didn't make it. But if our faith is still intact, then we made it. And our victory is a testimony to God's power that has strengthened us with might again and again to endure.

The second quality mentioned, patience, is so closely related to endurance, that the word could be translated "patiently enduring" or "longsuffering." But we often misinterpret longsuffering or patience to mean "putting up" with a problem that could and should be dealt with.

Sadly, mothers often think being patient means calmly taking a crayon from Johnny (who has written on Grandma's wall 12 times today) and saying, "Now we must not do that, Johnny." That is not being patient—that is being irresponsible. Patience sometimes means dealing with a problem appropriately time and time again. In fact, it could be called "patient action." And in Johnny's case, it would mean patiently swatting him 12 times, or putting him to bed 12 times, or making him sit in the corner 12 times, or doing whatever was necessary to stop him from writing on Grandma's wall.

And God's Spirit gives us the power to patiently deal with a problem again, and again. And without that power we have nothing to rely on but our own resources. Unfortunately in the area of patience and endurance, mankind is definitely limited—but the Christian is not when he steps out to be patient and endure relying on God to supply him the strength needed.

The third quality, joy, is a fruit of the Spirit, and also the natural product of thankfulness. There is no way you can experience joy unless you practice thankfulness. And 'thankfulness' in situations that require endurance and patience is your only hope for a happy, joyous Christian walk.

THE PRACTICAL POWER
TO BE STRENGTHENED, TO GRASP,
TO UNDERSTAND AND EXPERIENCE

The passage mentioning this power (Ephesians 3:16-21) is a favorite portion of the Bible for many, many Christians. And it states in the most dramatic way possible that God's love and power is beyond our imagination. It is so rich, it is almost overwhelming. And a complete book could be written on these 7 verses alone. But, in our study of the Spirit's practical power, we will focus on six points.

Point No. 1—Paul went to God in prayer and asked God's power for these Ephesian Christians. Power that could be supplied to them through the Spirit living within them.

Point No. 2—And one of the purposes of this power to enable Jesus Christ to dwell deep within their hearts. (This is a mystery mentioned in Colossians 1:26,27.) But the practical part to remember is: for Christ to dwell in their hearts required the strengthening of God through His Spirit.

Point No. 3—Next he petitioned God for power for all Christians to experience this so that all would be able to grasp how wide, long, high and deep God's love is.

Point No. 4—And he asked that we all experience this wide, long, high and deep love. Experience it in a way that goes beyond knowledge. And, consequently, we could all be filled and wholly flooded with God Himself.

Point No. 5—And it is possible for the Spirit's power at work within us, God can bring all of this about, and even far more—more than we can ask, or imagine. This passage is like space and eternity, it is too vast for our finite minds. We can understand what the words say, we can accept them—but which of us can truly comprehend them? But through the part we grasp, the experience we have of God's love, the fullness of God we receive, the Spirit can empower us to be conformed to the image of Christ.

THE CONCLUSION

The various functions of the Spirit in the Ministry of Practical Power are just different views of God's power in our lives through His Holy Spirit. And it is all based on faith from first to last.

And even though we looked at power formulas, they were nothing more nor less than well-thought-out steps of trusting faith.

DISCUSSION QUESTIONS

1. What point had the most impact on you in each section of the Spirit's Practical Power listed below:

   a) The Power to Hope
   b) The Power to Overcome
   c) The Power to Overcome Circumstances
   d) The Power to Glorify God
   e) The Power to Testify
   f) The Power to Endure and Be Patient With All Joy

The Spirit's Ministries For God's Children

Part 5
MINISTRY OF PARTNERSHIP

We have studied three ministries the Spirit has for us. The first required nothing on our part except the credentials of a Christian. The second required that we be open to God. The third ministry required a trusting faith. But the fourth ministry is different, it requires effort and submission on our part. In fact, it is a ministry of partnership. One the Spirit cannot fulfill without the cooperation of the believer in four areas: Living By the Spirit, Keeping In Step With the Spirit, Becoming Spirit Controlled, and Sowing to The Spirit.

LIVING BY THE SPIRIT

Living by the Spirit as mentioned in Galatians 5:16 is not spiritual life in the fast lane. On the contrary, it is the everyday excitement of the Christian walk. And Paul's description of it starts with one of its advantages, *"...So I say, live by the Spirit, and you will not gratify the desires of the sinful nature..."* Then he revealed the key for the direction of our lives. In verses 17,18, *"...For the sinful nature DESIRES what is contrary to the Spirit, and the Spirit what is contrary to the sinful nature. They are in conflict with each other..."*

From these verses and the use of the word "desire" we can see this warfare goes on in our minds. Satan knows this, so, he sees that we are brainwashed daily by books, movies, ads, tv programs, commercials, etc., etc., etc. designed to trigger thoughts and desires of the sinful nature. Desires that will grow into behaviors if we dwell on them.

Unfortunately, none of us can stop all sinful thoughts from flitting into our minds. But we can have a degree of control by censoring what we expose ourselves to: suggestive, sexy movies; immoral tv programs; pornographic literature, fantasies of wealth and power; and such like. These are simply Satan's visual aids, that he will bring to our mind time and again to tempt or entice us into the acts of the sinful nature.

But if we live by the Spirit, we will help the Spirit in conflict with the sinful nature by dwelling on the urgings or promptings the Spirit brings to mind: the remembrance of a favorite scripture, the desire or conviction to study God's Word, the wonder of God's creation, the urge to pray, the blessings of our lives, the comfort in fellowship, the thrill of a child's love, etc., etc. In this way, we can prevent the sinful nature from capturing the imagination of our hearts. And fulfill one of our obligations in our Ministry of Partnership with the Spirit.

KEEPING IN STEP WITH THE SPIRIT

To keep in step with the Spirit, it helps to understand the word translated "keeping in step" actually means "to proceed in a row, go in order" like marching. And the Spirit makes such marching in order possible by calling a cadence. We have all heard a cadence, "Hut, two, three, four...Hut, two, three, four." And those of us who have marched in a school band, drill team, etc. know its value. For a cadence makes it easier to keep in step with those in front, those in back and those beside you. And that is a major purpose of the Galatian passage (Galatians 5:13-26). Since we live by the Spirit, we should not only be keeping in step with the Spirit, we should also be keeping in step with EACH OTHER. In fact, in verse 13, Paul tells the Galatians they should be using their freedom from the Law, *"...to serve one another in love."* And then in verse 15 he said, *"...If you keep on biting and devouring each other, watch out or you will be destroyed by each other..."*

These Galatians, sadly, were not keeping in step with the Spirit. Because in the Spirit's cadence, there is fellowship and unity, not behaviors such as were mentioned in this passage: dissensions, bitings, devourings, conceit, envy and provocation. And just as their fellowship was disrupted by ungodly behaviors ours can be also.

And that situation develops when we hear the Spirit's cadence but ignore it, or fail to hear it at all. For the cadence of the Spirit is not a verbally heard cadence. Neither is it a 'felt' cadence. It is a cadence the Spirit has revealed and had recorded for us in the Word by God's prophets and Apostles. And if we are convinced we hear a verbal cadence or 'feel' a spiritual cadence, let us test it against the Word. For that is the only way we can 'know' it is from God. This has always been a problem with man (the desire to do his own thing) because in Proverbs we are told, *"...There is a way that SEEMETH right to a man, but the end thereof is death..."*

So, the cadence we hear and the direction we take must coincide exactly with scripture or it CANNOT be trusted. Otherwise, we could find ourselves marching to a different drummer (a deceitful one at that). So our responsibility to our partnership is to learn the Spirit's cadence, His whole cadence, not just rhythms that appeal to us individually. For we are not marching in an army of one. We are marching with the Spirit in a unified army of love and fellowship. And that army can only travel on the musical score of the Word.

BECOMING SPIRIT CONTROLLED

The Bible very clearly teaches how to be Spirit controlled and what that means in Romans 8:5-15. And it does so in one of the most assuring, comforting and exciting passages in the Bible. *"...Those who live according to their sinful nature have their minds set on what that nature desires; but those who live in accordance with the Spirit have their minds set on what the Spirit desires. The mind of sinful man is death, but the mind controlled by the Spirit is life and peace, because the sinful mind is hostile to God. It does not submit to God's law, nor can it do so. Those controlled by their sinful nature cannot please God..."* (Romans 8:5-7). The very first verse of this passage tells us how to be Spirit controlled. We must have our MIND SET on what the Spirit desires. That is the first step. Making a conscious decision based on commitment. It is more than an impulsive decision based on an emotional high or low. A mind set is much deeper, in fact, it could be compared to a 'holy stubbornness'.

Paul refers to the difference in those controlled by the sinful nature and those controlled by the Spirit. And states that difference is submission to God's law. But many people who do not follow God do not consider themselves 'hostile' to God. They explain, "I'm not against God. And I think some religion is good. But I just have a different life style. However, I'm as good as many people I see going to church all the time. And I can't believe God would send me to hell just because I don't go to church—not if He is as loving as they say." But the Roman passage only speaks of two categories, those who submit to God's laws and those who do not, there is no neutral territory.

This is understandable when you realize it is the yielding or submissive man to God that the Spirit CAN control or influence. So even those who do not consider themselves in opposition cannot be controlled by the Spirit—and consequently they ARE controlled by the powers of the sinful man. But if we are Spirit controlled by having our minds set on the things the Spirit desires, and submitting to God's laws, then we are Sons (vs. 15) and we do not have to be afraid to approach our God and call Him, "Daddy, Father."

SOWING TO THE SPIRIT

Galatians 6:7,8 speaks of sowing to the Spirit. It begins, *"...Do not be deceived: God cannot be mocked. A man reaps what he sows. The one who sows to please his sinful nature, from that nature will reap destruction; the one who sows to please the Spirit, from the Spirit will reap eternal life..."* This passage starts off with a warning. A warning that is a promise—we WILL reap what we sow (a universal principle). Then it makes a most enlightening observation: those who sow to please the sinful nature will reap destruction FROM THAT NATURE, while those who sow to please the Spirit FROM THE SPIRIT will reap eternal life. In other words, to nurture the sinful nature is literally to nurture destruction. And that truth is evident in our world every day.

When we meditate on this point we can see that to nurture the Spirit is to nurture eternal life. But how can we nurture God's Spirit? How can we sow to please Him—by providing for the Spirit the tools that give Him more influence in our lives:

(1) The First Tool is the Word—One reason they cannot be separated is obvious when you read Ephesians 6:17—The Spirit needs His Sword, which is the weapon in His hand to convict, direct, edify, and encourage us. And at the same time, we are providing for Him to take that weapon into our inner man. To be used during times of need to motivate, forbid, direct, admonish, exhort and encourage us.

Haven't we all been in situations that the right scripture comes to mind at just the right time. It may be a scripture that stops us in our tracks (a wise man forseeth evil and avoideth it) or gives us courage (God does not give us a spirit of fear but of power and love and self-control) or prevents us from reacting in anger (vengeance is mine saith the Lord). Unless we nurture the Spirit in the Word, we are handicapping His influence in our lives and handicapping our spiritual growth.

(2) The Second Tool is Faith—The stronger our faith, the stronger God's Spirit is in our lives. Not because our weak faith limits the might of God's power, but because our weak faith prevents us from stepping out to be empowered. Just as it does not motivate us to pray, to learn the Word, to love other Christians, to fellowship our brethren, to live lives of holiness.

There is only one way we can strengthen our faith, we must exercise it. And we start off easy by stretching to recall times God has rescued His people and then us as individuals. Then we must spend time 'experiencing' God by meditating on His love, His might, His strength, His power, His faithfulness. Next we must commune with God in prayer and praise. And just as there are no short-cuts to physical strength, there are no short-cuts to a strong faith. Particularly, at the beginning of our exercise program it may take strong discipline of our body and our mind, especially if we are out of spiritual shape. But the time will come that such exercise of faith will not be labor but the purest form of joy.

REAPING THE FRUIT OF THE SPIRIT

The result of living by the Spirit, keeping in step with the Spirit, being Spirit controlled and sowing to the Spirit is inevitable. The Fruit of the Spirit will first blossom in promise, then mature into the full-grown Fruit of the Spirit: love, joy, peace, patience, kindness, goodness, faithfulness, gentleness and self-control. But many Christians spend years in frustration and futility trying to develop the Fruit of the

Spirit. And they are doomed to failure. Because they have overlooked one of God's lessons from nature. We do not grow apples or pears or oranges—we grow trees that mature and produce apples or pears or oranges. In the same way we do not grow the Fruit of the Spirit. Instead we nurture the Spirit in our Ministry of Partnership by: (1) heeding the Spirit's promptings to dwell on...whatsoever things are true, whatsoever things are lovely, whatsoever things are pure, whatsoever things are admirable and praiseworthy. (2) by learning and listening to the Spirit's cadence of love and fellowship. (3) by setting our minds on what the Spirit desires and submitting to God's laws, and (4) by sowing to the Spirit in the Word, and in faith.

The result of which will be a glorious harvest of the Fruit of the Spirit year after year.

IN CONCLUSION

Many Christians walk victorious lives and never understand the power of The Spirit they live by. They are just walking by faith. And praise God it is so. Is it any wonder there was so much emphasis placed on faith in the scripture and very little explanation about how the power of the Spirit works. We would compare it to an experience most of us share daily. We all turn on switches, plug in electrical appliances, without the vaguest idea how electricity works. But our lack of knowledge does not stop it, as long as we have the faith to plug in and turn on the switch. But the person who does understand electricity, has a far greater respect, appreciation and confidence in its power. And understanding the power of the Spirit is like that. When we realize the power that is at work within us, we will step out in faith quicker to pursue our spiritual potential.

DISCUSSION QUESTIONS

1. What point had the most impact on you in each section of the Ministry of Partnership listed below:

   a) Living By The Spirit
   b) Keeping In Step With The Spirit
   c) Becoming Spirit Controlled
   d) Sowing to the Spirit

Bibliography

Barclay, William, *The Daily Study Bible,* The Letters to the Galatians and Ephesians, The Westminister Press: Philadelphia, PA, 1954.

Coffman, Burton J., *Commentary on Galatians, Ephesians, Philippians, Colossians,* Firm Foundation Publishing House: Austin, TX, 1977.

Floyd, Harvey, *Is The Holy Spirit For Me?,* 20th Century Christian, Inc.: Nashville, TN, 1981.

Jewett, P. K., *Encyclopedia of the Bible,* The Holy Spirit, Zondervan: Grand Rapids, MI, 1975.

Nee, Watchman, *Spiritual Reality or Obsession,* Christian Fellowship Publishers, Inc.: New York, NY, 1970.

Nygren, Anders, *Commentary on Romans,* Fortress Press: Philadelphia, PA, 1949.

Ogilvie, Lloyd John, *Drumbeat of Love,* Word, Inc.: Waco, TX, 1976.

Rogers, Richard, *The Holy Spirit,* Sentinel Publishing: Lubbock, TX, 1968.

Thomas, J.D., *The Spirit and Spirituality,* Biblical Research Press: Abilene, TX, 1966.